I Never Wanted to Set the World on Fire

But Now That I'm 50, Maybe It's a Good Idea!

Bob Basso, Ph.D.

Seaside Press

Library of Congress Cataloging-in-Publication Data

Basso, Bob.
  I never wanted to set the world on fire: but now that I'm 50, maybe it's
  a good idea! / by Bob Basso.
     p.   cm.
  ISBN 1-55622-387-0
  1. Midlife crisis--Case studies.   2. Life change events--Psychological
  aspects--Case studies.   3. Basso, Bob.   I. Title.
  BF724.65.M53B37   1995
  155.6'6'092--dc20
                                                                94-48651
                                                                CIP

Seaside Press is an imprint of Wordware Publishing, Inc.
No part of this book may be reproduced in any form or by
any means without permission in writing from
Wordware Publishing, Inc.

Printed in the United States of America

ISBN1-55622-387-0
10 9 8 7 6 5 4 3 2 1
9505

All inquiries for volume purchases of this book should be addressed
to Wordware Publishing, Inc., at 1506 Capital Avenue, Plano, Texas
75074. Telephone inquiries may be made by calling:
(214) 423-0090

Contents

Looking Back. . .

On June 20, 1989, I put my career as a keynote speaker and management consultant on hold and took up temporary residence in a treehouse at the eighteen-mile marker on the east end of the tiny island of Molokai, in the Hawaiian Islands.

Why?

It was something Dr. Dan said at my annual physical after carefully inventorying several newly arrived ailments: "You're suffering from what we call 'general malaise.' "

malaise—(ma-lz; Fr. ma-lez) n. (Fr.; mal, bad + aise, ease) A vague feeling of physical discomfort or uneasiness, as before an illness.

Vague feeling, hell! The shooting pains in the chest, the perpetual migraine, the refusal to accept the mall as the center of the universe, the urge to throw a grenade in the front seat of every automobile with one of those damn atomic blasting car stereos, not to mention total repulsion for acid rain, the melting of the polar ice caps, holes in the ozone, every "How To" book on the market, relationships as an epidemic, gridlock, mail order catalogs, and everything on prime time TV were all very specific! Funny, when you were thirteen they called it "growing pains." Now that you're fifty plus, they call it "general malaise."

"We'll take tests," said the red-cheeked Dick Clark look-alike internist.

So they took tests.

I didn't wait around for the results.

One of the pluses of suddenly being fifty is you completely reject adulthood, lose all respect for outside authority, and start listening to the little heart-voice within. I was all ears. It said, "Go to Molokai. Push the pause button. Do nothing. Listen for further instructions. Little voice, over and out."

I went.

I kept a diary . . . of sorts. When the little voice spoke, I wrote. It spoke in the middle of some of the wildest, most pleasantly absurd times of my life. Answers came in the form of adventure, folly, nature, midnight nudity, sex, conversations with Jack London and Henry David Thoreau, and a very instructive relationship with a maverick cat named John Muir. I'm also certain I was the beneficiary of several suspected whispers from the Almighty.

As I look back, I suppose I was taking a seventh-inning stretch, perhaps in search of a mid-course correction, looking for a hole in the clouds to dash through and abandon all this New Age techno-yuppie madness, with its obsessive dependency on nonessentials.

My post-World War II world of hope, pride, family values, and black-and-white movies with happy endings was over. It would never return.

I suspect all "fifty-pluses" have to face up to that jarring new reality. No, it can't be explained away as a "second mid-life crisis" or the simple culture shock of clashing generations. It's much deeper than that. It's a primal struggle to validate that life itself still has meaning. It's a fifty-plus need to answer a simple question that is at the very heart and soul of our future civilization—are we just changing ballparks, or are we actually changing the game?

I'm not sure that what I learned in my treehouse will help any other confused mid-lifer answer those questions, but if my experiences—sometimes wacky, sometimes profound, but always instructive—spark an interest to search out your own treehouse, real or imagined, I will feel my time spent on these pages was eminently serviceable. Enjoy!

Bob Basso

"When I was fifty, I realized heaven had a mind of its own."

Confucius

"In middle age there is mystery. There is mystification."

John Cheever, author

"Fifty is God's way of saying 'Stop taking yourself so seriously.' You're not that important. Just remember, when you die, ultimately, the size of your funeral will depend on the weather."

Janet Basso,
author's mother

1

I Never Expected Sex at 35,000 Feet, But . . . There It Was

TWA 403 from Los Angeles to Honolulu was the first leg of my flight to freedom. Like Candide, Gauguin, Thoreau, and Lord Jim, I was leaving the madness of modern life with the relative certitude I was going to a better place—a tiny, idyllic island in the South Pacific where honesty, nonviolence, and appreciation for a good Guy Lombardo tune was still possible.

I hated to admit it, but the reality was stark, immediate, and overwhelming. I was fifty years old, and nothing in America looked familiar to me anymore—the music, the movies, families, the starting lineup of the New York Mets, nothing. Not even the in-flight meal—a yellow-green mushy patty with scattered red blotchy dots that could either be red onion or an unknown killer fungus. My 300-plus-pound female seating companion, with the name "Franny" embroidered across the green and white stripes on her sumo-size left breast, read my confusion and volunteered, "It's vegetarian quiche. This airline is very de rigueur." Her laughter shook both our seats.

I closed my eyes and ran pictures of Molokai Island across my mental screen ... lush valleys with 400-foot waterfalls cascading onto glittering sandy beaches ringing a land that time graciously forgot.

My intent was not to make conversation of any sort with any human being until I had reached my final destination. But that ended when I decided to stretch my legs in the galley space between first class and tourist.

The Lady in Blue asked me if I would stand guard at the door of the john because the lock was broken. Her name was Patrella, twenty-three or twenty-four maybe, with glistening ebony hair, a sensual centerfold body in a skintight navy blue dress that had every pair of male eyes boiling with lustful possibilities. A small white button sat in the crescent of her bulging cleavage, "Save The Whales." I've never been more aroused by an ecological issue in my life. I was suddenly alive with a young man's passion.

Many not-so-funny voices come calling when you hit fifty. The first arrives just before you are about to blow out the last candle on the surprise birthday cake. It is the loudest and it sticks around the longest. It repeats the same satanic message over and over again. It finally wedges itself in your subconscious right next to that damn forty-foot neon warning sign: "It's a fact that more men die of heart attacks in their fifties than at any other age. Be ready!" The voice, which sounds strangely like David Brinkley, says, "If you haven't made it by now, you'll never make it. Time is running out." It may be the devil's greatest propaganda, because you suddenly find yourself preoccupied with a whole schedule of bizarre rituals, like timing how long it takes you to get an erection; combing your hair from the back to the front; charting your irregularity to see if a deadly pattern is developing; taking your blood pressure every time you go to the drugstore; looking for incontrovertible proof of life after death; and becoming an expert on everything to do with your prostate gland. On top of all this, there's a pesky army of cross-examining agitators constantly screaming those ultimate questions at you: "What do you do that's meaningful when the dream dies?" "Did you ever really pursue your joy?" "Should you have listened to your mother and taken a secure civil service job, like the mailman?" All these faceless horsemen gallop through your thoughts seeding chaos and pushing all your unrequited hopes and fading promise into yesterday's shadows. A giant clock is ticking. You're fifty, and the warranty on immortality has suddenly expired. You feel it conclusively in every unexplained ache and shortness of breath.

What to do?

The spirit seems to say, "Seek God in nature." The flesh says, "Make it with a younger woman. Real young."

I've always thought that was a pitifully false refuge for aging men seeking to beat death by bonding with youth. But now I'm fifty, and the voice of conscience isn't so rigid and assured anymore. What was once heresy may now be holistic. Who knows? Hell, it may even be a rite of passage. I didn't invent the idea. It just seemed to naturally evolve along with the receding hairline, the stiff joints, and the curve ball that doesn't break anymore.

I thought if the situation did present itself to me, it would have to be a seventeen-year-old petite nymphet named Candy or Morningstar coming up to me after a college lecture and suggesting she get to know my wonderful mind better by inviting me to have some herbal tea with her in front of a roaring fire at her deaf parents' hunting lodge while they slept soundly three floors above.

I was wrong. It's happening now, 35,000 feet above the Pacific, in front of the tourist class john.

We talk.

Patrella is one part kook, one part shrewd entrepreneur (she owns a thriving futon furniture and design business in Carmel, California), and one part genuine defender of the environment. She is refreshingly direct and totally unencumbered by sentence structure. She never bothers to connect thoughts.

"I'm on a ten-day camping trip to a remote part of Hawaii you probably never heard of, Molokai. Well, it's really not a camping trip, it's a gathering of like minds to center our beings with the flow of the planet. Last year we met at Dacca, Bangladesh. I hope you don't mind chatting with me. I really don't want to go back to my seat. Everybody's looking at my boobs. That's very shallow, don't you think? Did you know Madam Curie was Polish? I read that in the in-flight magazine. I have a good friend who's a volcanologist. He's convinced me that the world as we know it started with a volcanic eruption that produced Molokai forty to forty-five million years ago. I feel like I'm going home."

During one of her infrequent pauses for a breath, I fill her in on my mid-life retreat to the woods.

"Gee, you don't look that old. How old are you?"

"I'm . . . forty-one."

She smiles and feels my right bicep.

"But you're solid. You take care of yourself. I like that in a mature man." She feels my other bicep.

I throw her a little test. Does she have a sense of humor? I've always pictured my youthful fantasy lady and I laughing a lot before, during, and after. I figure that's the only way a good Catholic can justify such lascivious adventure.

"I think you'd better stop there, Patrella. If you feel any of my other muscle groups, you're going to send 120 male passengers into cardiac arrest."

She laughs uproariously. The fantasy begins.

A few hours later on the ground, she picks up her khaki camouflaged backpack from the luggage carousel, gives me a one-armed hug and says, "I'll visit you in your treehouse." She flashes me a Betty Grable pin-up poster wink, touches my face gently, and disappears into the crowd.

Was Miss Patrella, the futon lady from Carmel, a phantasm, a construct of fading hope, or is the fickle god Eros finally giving me my shot at immortality?

My loins don't care. They are about to set off the airport sprinkler system. I thought I was turning my back on the world, the flesh, and the devil, but if the dreamy Miss P returns as promised, I just may have to settle for two out of three . . . for the time being.

2

My Life in a Tree Begins

I arrive.

Something's wrong . . . but right. It's yesterday, a long time ago.

I feel it.

The bumpy, twin-engine, prop-driven Hawaiian Airlines plane was a clever deception, that's it. It was, in fact, a time machine left at the inter-island air terminal at precisely the same time I was to leave for Molokai. I somehow wandered into its well-worn, gray belly obviously guided by a mysterious force that only attracts recent AARP[1] card holders. It gave all the appearance of flying east by southeast from Oahu for eighteen minutes over the temperamental white-capped Kaiwi Channel and then making a silky-smooth landing at the Lilliputian Hoolehua airport—sleepy, rustic, unobtrusive tenant on a shamrock green sliver between two hulking mountains.

All an illusion.

---

1   American Association of Retired Persons

It's definitely yesterday, 1940-something. Where else would the wind gently muffle the sounds of modern commerce. Where else would you see such old wooden baggage carts, a barefooted handler sound asleep, knotty pine ballpark benches in the open-air lobby, rattan furniture, and a clock twenty-one minutes slow. No control tower. No metal detectors or X-ray machines in sight. No regimentation. No signs. No hassle. No hustle. Past the tiny three-table sawdust-on-the-floor bruised mahogany bar. Wait a minute. I'm sure I saw Raymond Chandler, or was it Dashiel Hammet, downing a straight bourbon at that end table. Maybe not. Either way, it's their type of joint.

The brown-skinned wahine at the Tropical rent-a-car counter is a magician. She's warming her baby's bottle, rocking the under-the-desk cradle, balancing two phones on her shoulders, straightening out some confusion over tonight's canoe race practice for both listeners while flawlessly processing my reservation.

She points to my car in the lot across the way. I'm expecting a '32 Chevy stick-on-the-floor complete with a rumble seat. I get a dented combat-veteran '85 Toyota covered waist-high in volcanic red dirt. Yesterday fades.

The magician smiles apologetically. "Sor-ree. We're short-handed. Our lot boy has a volleyball tournament today. I'll take fifteen percent off your bill."

Up the red hill, eight miles past the family farms, a dozen different storybook wooden-framed steepled churches side by side, past the legendary Coconut Grove of King Kamehameha V with its thousand-plus coconut palms planted in 1803—considered a special resting place of the Gods—and into Molokai's principal town, Kaunakakai. It's yesterday again. Old Tucson, circa

1910. Three blocks of false-front stores that could easily have found their way into a John Ford Western epic. Names like Hop Inn, Imamura's Dry Goods, The Friendly Market, and Mid-Nite Inn dominate. Old men, mostly retired Filipino cane field workers, sit on benches and exchange tales, stopping only to pay an admiring silent tribute to a passing young lady. Folks shop and gather in small groups to laugh and hug a lot. An old lady with a giant hibiscus in her hair sells fruit from the back of her '52 Plymouth. No traffic lights, so drivers stop and smilingly wave pedestrians across the street.

Molokai is the old Hawaii of Jack London, Robert Louis Stevenson, and Somerset Maugham—unhurried, quiet, at peace with itself—everywhere a common reverence for serenity.

Well, not everywhere.

A souped-up green Volkswagen with balloon tires and yellow racing stripes comes screeching into town, car stereo blasting at sonic boom levels. The unconcerned teenage driver with the heavy-metal scowl and jet black wraparound sunglasses seems more symbolic than real. A harbinger of the inevitable seduction of modern life. His ugly volume is rattling the tin roof of Malia's craft store. Old men stop talking. The hugging and laughing stops. The hibiscus lady puts her hands over her ears. They all stare and shake their heads, but nobody does anything about it. Obviously Molokians are no different than any Polynesian people. They're genetically unable to assert their displeasure with the white man's devils. Well, I didn't come 2,500 miles to a South Pacific hideaway to have my communication with nature shattered by some orange-haired mutant and his concert from hell.

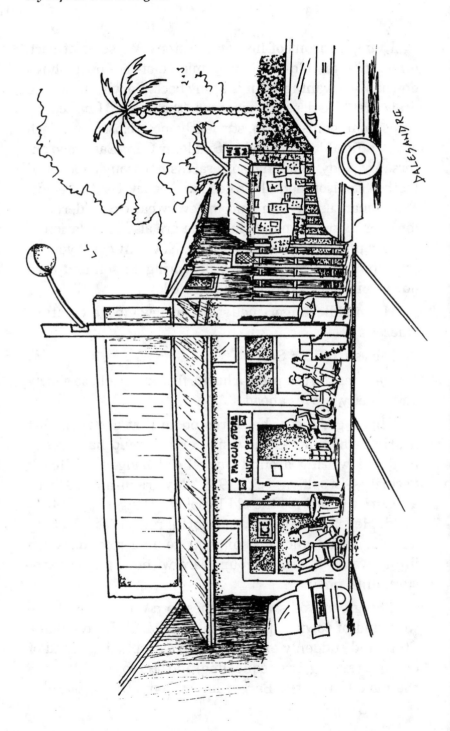

I jump in front of his car. He stops. We stare at each other. It's an old-fashioned, middle-of-the-town show-down. My advantage. Sun's at my back. So who's going to draw first? He does. He gives me "the finger." I match his greasy, antagonistic grin, stridently move closer, and flash a very official-looking badge. Suddenly Clint Eastwood en-ters my body, pushing soft sarcasm through clenched teeth. "Environmental Protection Agency, South Pacific. Young man, aside from ignoring every basic consideration for your fellow human beings, you are also in violation of every sound ordinance in the state. Now why don't you try something radical—be a decent, caring person and turn down your noise box to a reasonable level."

His middle finger melts and a new, docile creature emerges.

"Yes sir, officer. Sorry."

He gives the gas pedal a butterfly tap and oh, so slowly and quietly, moves ahead.

Thank goodness the stereo boom that destroyed his hearing also blurred his vision or he would have easily read the writing around my official badge—"Ballpark Security—Brooklyn, N.Y., 1938." My grand-uncle Al was a security guard for the old Brooklyn Dodgers at Ebbets Field. He left me a legacy of colorful memories watching legends at play and this shiny badge. I've carried it deep in my wallet for thirty-four years without public expo-sure, until now.

The green Volkswagen comes to a quiet stop at the west end of town opposite the Molokai Fish and Game Store and suddenly explodes in an ear-splitting blend of engines revving, tires squealing, and stereo convulsing to the max. Conan the Barbarian Jr. floors the accelerator and disappears in a sooty haze of smoke, middle finger defiantly extended high over the roof of his psychedelic war wagon.

Too bad Uncle Al didn't leave me his gun.

I drop into Friendly Isle Realty to pick up the key and sign the paperwork for my treehouse.

Kolola, the soft-spoken agent sitting behind a koa dish of fresh mangoes, smiles.

"There's no key."

"How come?" I reply.

"No lock," says she. "It's open. Send the check when you're ready."

A hundred yards past the eighteen-mile marker on the southern coast road, there it is—my Walden Pond. Up on a grassy knoll overlooking the feisty Kalohi Channel separating Lanai and Maui is a little yellow-and-brown shack set immediately behind a forty-foot-high mango tree in full bloom. So close behind it gives the illusion of actually sitting halfway up and in the middle of the tree. I accept the illusion. It's offically a treehouse.

Down below on the other side of the road is a mile-long stretch of silky white sand beach dotted with petrified mangroves. Their chalky white, serpentine limbs climb out of the sand, combining with the shadows of approaching nightfall to form a ghostlike reminder of twisted metal hulks of war rusting in the surf, proud casualties of a massive amphibious assault long, long ago. My imagination flies. I name it "Omaha Beach[2]."

---

2   Famed landing site of American troops at the 1944 D-Day, Normandy beachhead.

Inside the Treehouse

My new escape from the modern age is Spartan but functional. A fifteen-by-five-foot screen-enclosed lanai (porch) offers a 180-degree view of the Pacific found only in midsummer night's dreaming, or on one of those Franklin Mint Limited Edition Collector Plates. Inside is a combination airy bedroom-living room-kitchen, with all the modern conveniences of post-Depression rural America. There's a first edition Sears & Roebuck front-loading toaster that will also double as an oven; a rusty, breadbox-size refrigerator that hasn't been defrosted since the Truman administration; and a temperamental commode that, I will come to discover, only flushes at its own command . . . usually between 1:00 and 3:00 in the morning.

I unpack my only two obligations—The College Edition of Webster's Dictionary and the Douy-Rheims version of the Bible, both graduation gifts from my Dad, the fire chief, who said I could never be truly educated until I've read both, cover to cover. I will.

I also have an ancient thirty-five-pound Royal manual typewriter, a prized ringside relic of the 1923 Dempsey-Firpo fight, a three-month supply of paper, my old baseball mitt with the horsehair stuffing, a half-dozen music cassettes of "The Best of the Forties," a copy of Mark Twain's *Life on the Mississippi,* an anthology of Thoreau and Emerson, assorted works of Jack London, and about fifty yellowing copies of *Ladies' Home Journal* magazine left by the former occupant. From the fashion look of the underwear ads, I'd say circa 1950.

I'm well equipped to do nothing and grow.

3

The Learning Starts . . . Changing the Names of Monsters Is a Lot Easier on the Heart

Sitting alone in a treehouse writing, reading, thinking, listening, and watching the infinite swirling patterns of the Pacific, you become aware of a startling compulsion—you must make friends with all other living things. It's not an intellection. It's an instinct. It's not to be explained. It just is. Nature teaches us all we need to know to survive the flow of the seasons, and this lesson is overwhelmingly immediate. You become an Indian. You get quiet and let the unchanged essences of nature push and pull you to a valid way of living. You know when to rise in the morning. When to work. When to rest. When to let go of all thinking and just float on your back. You respond only to the chemistry of your own body, and it always seems to be right. And without all the excess city baggage, you discover being friendly is a natural thing to be.

Something else happens in the woods. You become a kid, constitutionally, in fact. Emerson said, "In the woods, a man casts off his years as the snake his slough, and at what period soever of life is always a child . . . the woods is perpetual youth . . . in the woods we return to reason and faith."

And it is essentially more reasonable out here for the child in you to follow the path of Doctor Doolittle rather than Attila the Hun. You relate to all things. Nothing is inanimate anymore. You find yourself talking to everybody and everything. You talk to the bed, to the fence post, to the wind, to low flying clouds, to the mailbox, and to the animals. I do.

And the animals talk back. All of them, that is, but one, a certain Mister John Muir, the most cantankerous, ornery, cold, independent, selfish cuss I have ever known.

Just writing his name frazzles my nerve endings. I'd better start with the others first.

The Diving Santini Brothers visit twice a day, usually with the rise and fall of the sun. Romulus and Remus Santini are cocky, yellow-beaked mynah birds who think they're P-38 dive bombers. In the middle of a lazy flight from one tree limb to another, they will suddenly veer off and crash dive into any manner of living thing they feel is invading their domain. I've watched them zoom into dogs, big and small, cows, roosters, goats, donkeys, and poor old Mister Buelli, the yard man. They never draw blood. They're content to just make statements—"This is my land, beat it!" For the price of some whole-wheat bread crumbs on the porch sill, they will abandon their combative ways, put on their showbiz hats, and do what mynahs do extraordinarily well—mimic the sounds of

others. Romy and Remy are the best. Their pigeon trill is
superior, but they do a pretty fair blackbird yelp as well.
We usually talk at dusk under the lilikoi tree on the side of
the house. I ask them why they are always so hyper about
everything they do. Romy, who always pauses before an-
swering any question, struts around à la Jimmy Cagney,
stops, cocks his head, does his W.C. Fields laugh—you
know the one that sounds like a Model T backfiring in a
tunnel—and says, "Mynah birds, like all birds, only do
what is necessary. And if you've got to do necessary things,
you might as well do it with enthusiasm and energy. It
makes the day mean something." At least I think that's
what he said. Mynah birds talk in a very low whisper.

Donaghy, the vegetarian sneak, is a gray-tailed mongoose.[1] He's a fruit thief with no allegiance to history. His
forebears were brought to Hawaii in 1883 to make the
highly destructive cane field rat their number one entrée.
No one is sure just how well they accomplished that
chore, but we do know they keep their appetite focused
on meat, filling their long, narrow bellies with a steady
diet of native geese and other local birds. All of them except Donaghy. He's a New Age mongoose. No red meat.
He hides behind the big drooping banana leaf at the side
of the treehouse waiting for Mr. Buelli, an affable slow-
moving yard man, to gather his half-dozen ripened
mangoes and neatly line them up on the running board
of his old flatbed trunk. When Mr. B. disappears behind
the house to rake leaves and cut down the brush, out
saunters Donaghy. He walks very slowly, lest the Diving

---

1   Ferret-like mammal resembling a squirrel, noted for their ability to kill
     poisonous snakes, rodents, etc.

Santinis spot him and crash dive into his buns, which they have done on several painful occasions. He deceptively zigzags his way to the running board, jumps up, knocks two of the ripest mangoes to the ground, lies on his back, rolls a mango onto his stomach, and feasts. I suspect his uncustomary eating position is to keep the circling Santinis in sight in case of an aerial attack. I've seen him put away three fat mangoes at one sitting, darn near the equivalent of his own weight.

For some strange reason, Donaghy, the fruit connoisseur, who's also supposed to be high-strung and anti-human, responds to my call and routinely slithers over to eat green peppers, pineapple chunks, and sesame spaghetti from my hand. He usually does all the talking. I rarely get a word in edgewise. But when I do, I pump him about his non-mongoose ways, like eating fruit and living under a palm frond instead of burrowing an apartment deep into the red clay like the rest of his species. He grinds his beaver-like front teeth, wets his lips, and rambles on about taking risks, pushing traditional and genetic limits in order to discover new things. Once when I was sitting under the lichee tree, alongside the mango tree, reading a little Thoreau, he told me, "A tree can only be a tree and stand so tall and give so much shade. A wave can never be more than a swirling mass of water. But if you're breathing, you've got an edge. You can become more than you are, try a new menu, eat fruit, and sleep in a cool place."

"Yeah," I replied. "But every time you try something new you run the risk of getting bit in the buns."

I don't think mongooses can sigh, but Donaghy came awfully close, then replied, "Hey, most of life's problems have no solutions, just trade-offs. Besides, there's always a price to pay when you run ahead of the herd."

He finished off my dry roasted cashew nuts, rolled over on his back, and took a nap.

I resumed reading Thoreau's brilliant essay in defense of the militant abolitionist John Brown: "No man in America has ever stood up so persistently and effectively for the dignity of human nature, knowing himself for a man, and the equal of any and all governments. In that sense he was the most American of us all."

Other friends are Mert and Marge, inseparable retired veterans and frequent visitors from the next farm. They always seem quite content to let me babble on about life, love, and receding hairlines without interruption . . . two rusty old fireplugs with stubby feet, liver spots, and expanding potbellies. Mert and Marge are two heavily scarred, wild boar-hunting dogs who have beaten the odds on life expectancy for their profession. In the old days they would hunt out the savage 300-pound saw-toothed pigs that roam the Kamakou mountains behind us and perform the least appreciated bravery in outdoor sports. It was their job to corner their deadly adversary in the open field and charge him from two different angles—one grabbing the throat, while the other partner had the less desirable task of locking onto the boar's testicles, restraining the enraged beast fore and aft while the hunter moved in and cut the boar's throat. (From the constant sour expression on Mert's face, it was obvious which end he was responsible for.) It is the highest form of teamwork in the bloody world of hunting. The hunter trusts his dogs will not let go despite excruciating pain as the crazed boar repeatedly sinks his six-inch-long, razor-sharp teeth into their flanks and wildly flings them against the ground in a furious fight to the death. The dogs trust the hunter to move swiftly and find the jugular on the first thrust before they're overpowered by the beast's rage.

The good dogs last a year or two, usually dying in combat. The few great ones get to stick around long enough to retire on a small pension, which includes chasing cars, swimming in the mud flats, and letting the hunter's kids pretend they're longhorn cattle and lasso them in the front yard. Mert and Marge are beyond all that. They're hall-of-famers. They sleep in a store-bought doghouse, eat three balanced meals a day, keep their own agenda, and have carte blanche to visit any part of the island. But mostly they just play, rest a lot, and follow me on my long walks along Omaha Beach at dusk. We can sit at the abandoned hermit's shack beyond the mangroves for thirty or forty minutes without a word, just watching another flaming sunset close the chapter on another great day in the tropics. On those rare occasions when they do talk, it's always the same theme, "Don't just be a dog. Become an expert at something, then play a lot."

Now we come to that no-good, self-centered, detached little snob, John Muir.

Why do I call him that when he's a lot shorter than his famous namesake, considerably less hirsute under the chin, and has positively never set foot in the Sierras or even heard about Yosemite? Because I am an inheritor of a long family tradition of giving all life's monsters noble or silly names that immediately seem to reduce the evil they can work on you. I think it's the sound of calamity that does the most damage. Don't you think more people would survive CANCER if we renamed it "Fa-la-la-la," or hold together a lot better during a HEART ATTACK if the doc said, "No problem, you're just having a little 'Oopee Whoop' "? Renaming monsters changes the perception of pain. Ask any "Sanitary Engineer" who used to be a "Garbage Man." It doesn't make the garbage disappear. It just changes how you feel about it. Maybe in the long run all we can do is change how we react to garbage. I think words that make you smile can't hurt you. Okay, there are some monsters that deserve evil-sounding names like poverty, pollution, PMS, and junk mail. But that's about it. John Muir is a dirty brown, tiger-striped cat who lives under my treehouse.

For starters, I've been a dog man all my life, so any attempt at a relationship with this critter is no easy matter. John is the embodiment of all the black myths you've ever heard about his kind. You look into those steely green eyes and you know this self-assured furry little stoic is a mystic, a soul reader. He knows immediately who you really are, what you are. And that damn expressionless little face with the frozen smugness . . . I hate it.

He knows the answers, and I don't. And he knows I know he knows, and that drives me nuts.

So why don't I just ignore him altogether? Because when you live in the woods, you not only need to be friendly with the animals, you also need their approval. You need to be accepted as an equal. You need to feel your slack city ways haven't disqualified you from being a part of the basic, more meaningful dominion of nature. And there's no democracy out here. You need a unanimous vote of the tribe to be voted in. I lack one vote.

He sits exactly fifteen feet away from me (I've measured the distance) on the porch sill and watches me type every day. He'll sit for hours, just staring at my two-finger key banging with no apparent editorial comment. And no matter how many times I attempt to move closer, he adjusts the distance, and we end up fifteen feet apart. I've tried everything to lessen the distance between us— rubbed my face with honey and played dead on the front lawn, whispered kind words, smiled, hummed, sang, whistled, cajoled, bargained, and begged. Nothing. I've tried treating him like an equal . . . chatting off-handedly about Hegelian utilitarianism, the junk bond market, and Henry Adams' observation that the succession of presidents from Washington to Grant was in itself enough to disprove Darwin's theory of evolution. No response. I've offered to be a good neighbor and give him a lift into town, invited him to take a jog with me to the twenty-mile marker or do some light aerobics on the porch. Nothing. Just the same fifteen feet of indifference.

Today I invoke some classical Adam Smith supply and demand. I put a little supply of 2% low-fat milk in a tin plate and leave it in plain sight of his nesting place. I sit down by the offering in anticipation of our first close personal contact. Ah, there he is, peeking out from behind the trunk of the plumeria tree, but no movement. I will not budge. We sit and stare at each other for thirty-five minutes. I time it. Nothing. I budge and move back a little. Nothing. Dammit! I move back a little further, about fifteen feet. Slowly, his primordial demand for calcium overcomes his acquired fear of Brooklyn-Italians living in treehouses, and he cautiously moves to the peace offering, devours it handily, licks his chops, and arrogantly scampers back up the tree.

Ah, but it's only a matter of time, John, before we erase this five-yard gap of mistrust, for I have just learned a new truth. Even in the forest primeval, everybody has his price. Cats are people, too.

4

Do Country Stores Have Souls?

I'm getting restless depending solely on my third-degree flat feet for transportation. Relative isolation has its joys, but when you live on a tropical island, you are immediately overwhelmed by an ancient curiosity—you've got to explore, move out and about through tide pools, clay pits, gullies, water caves, and gothic rock formations. You've got to touch every part of your island, because this is where nature is most instructive. This is where land, sea, and sky converge to conclusively prove there is order, beauty, and balance in the universe, and if you only get off your duff and touch some of it, you will find magic. There are no hieroglyphics in nature, just simple answers. I want some.

My three-day Tropical car rental contract has long expired. I need more mobility. How?

I do like the early Hawaiians . . . I wait for a moonlit night, go down to the beach, and ask the great 'aumakua (god) for relief. True to the custom of the ancients, I leave an offering to stimulate the mana (spirit) of the deities. I sit for an hour watching the high tide carry my half-pack of sesame spaghetti, wrapped tightly in banana leaves, out to the shipping lanes beyond the reef. If my newly found respect for Polynesian culture and spirituality has any substance, an answer will come.

It does . . . sort of.

The next day, on my pre-dawn walk up the coast, I follow Mert and Marge as they rummage through an abandoned fisherman's hut slowly sinking into the mud flats at the twenty-mile marker. Forty-pound retired boar hunters are too little to upset the delicate balance of the angel-hair-thin rotting floorboards, but one 200-pound, graying biped thrashing around the salt-encrusted jet-sam and flotsam of this seaside antiquity has the effect of King Kong entering a house of cards. First, a creaking noise like an old wooden ship running aground, then a giant rumble, followed by the whole left side of the shanty collapsing, sending the rusted slivers of the tin roof sliding into the thick keawe bushes hugging the shoreline. Abandon ship! Mert and Marge leap through a hole in the crumbling floor and ride the current downstream to safety.

I grab the last standing two-by-four support beam and manage to survive the quake with nothing more than a harmless shower of sand, rotting lilikoi (passion fruit), and a batch of waterlogged *Life* Magazines, circa 1952. I salvage one with a smiling President Ike Eisenhower waving at his inaugural parade audience. This is not a fitting resting place for the designer of the Normandy invasion.

Amid the rubble, my prayers are answered.

I am now free to explore the Molokai beyond my limited horizon. The spirit has wings; the body has a bicycle.

Well, technically a bicycle, practically more like a work in progress from Fred Flintstone's garage—a seatless, rusted frame sitting on little more than faith and two mismatched patched tires. The handlebars are frozen in the extreme up position like the ones on those super-dude Harley Davidson motorcycles. Brakes never entered the mind of the designer, and two twisted rods are all that's left of the pedals, but, to a footsore treehouse dweller, this is a late model Astin Martin. Mert comes back and pees on the back tire. In my new sense of spiritual renewal, I take it as a sign of nature's blessing.

Lots of sanding, patching, and oiling, and the darn thing still looks pretty awful, but it does produce locomotion and a new world of possibilities.

One of those possibilities is the fact that I may forget my chariot of fire is seatless and absentmindedly sit down, giving myself a surprise proctological probe of epic proportions from the rusted, pointy support rod. I'll worry about it tomorrow.

Tomorrow is another sun-drenched gem in the tropics. A big juicy papaya from the tree on the side, two mangoes from the tree of life, and a banana from the patch out back. Voilà! Instant breakfast.

Half a tin of 2% for John Muir, a quick swim down at Omaha Beach, and I'm ready for my morning reading. Who will it be today . . . Twain, Maugham, Thoreau, or Wil and Ariel Durant's *History of Western Thought* . . . No, none of them. What's wrong with me? Fifty-year-old men need motion, not reflection. There's no more wisdom or insight in words when you get to this age, only in experience, doing, feeling, reaching, working your joints. Mahatma Ghandi was right when he concluded at age fifty that all the philosophy from all the world's great thinkers doesn't add up to the knowledge one derives from a simple, single act of unbounded joy. However evil the world may seem, there is always the possibility of a single act of joy by doing. And within that act you have all the basic knowledge you need for healthy survival. Ghandi was right. More doing than thinking. Have you ever seen a thin philosopher? Never. They're too busy vegetating in their Lazy Boy recliners analyzing instead of doing. Not for me, no sir. Don't think. Do. To bike! Ride, ride, you son of nature. You're 2,374 miles from the nearest gridlocked freeway. Revel in that freedom.

Off I go, pedaling in a standing position, down America's most beautifully perfumed highway, Molokai coastal road 470. Why the number I don't know, because it's the only coastal road on the island. And what a road, trellised in sweet-smelling frangipani, vanda orchids, eucalyptus, and a dozen more exotic odors wafting down from the creased south face of the Kamakou mountain range. Past neatly painted mailboxes with colorful floral art and island names that sing the ethnic rhythms of the Pacific—Mapeul, Keliikipi, Babayan, Sakurada, Laufalemana, Wong, and Pagaduan.

It's amazing how a few inches of elevated smooth-wheeled propulsion can dramatically transform your perspective on the world. You're passing by the same scenes you've passed on foot a hundred times, but the reality is somehow different. Maybe it's becoming part of a grander motion . . . the awareness that you, that everything ultimately is in constant motion, and that motion has a natural synchronicity to it. You just can't find it

walking, jogging, or squatting behind an internal com-
bustion engine. You need to move at the speed of the
wind, the kind of moderated speed you can only get on a
bicycle.

I'm sure the synchronicity would be even sweeter if
only I could sit down. Ah, well, every unbounded joy has
its trade-offs.

The easy flowing pattern of genteel, dilapidated local
plantation houses with their tin roofs, open lanais, and col-
orfully improvised add-ons are occasionally and abruptly
broken by the foreign intrusion of modern construction—
prefabricated pricey boxes with the mandatory wraparound porches, tinted windows, and cathedral ceilings.
The parade of mainland malcontents is on.

It's happening all over the Pacific from Molokai to
Cook Island to the Marquesas and New Zealand. A whole
new class of displaced persons is on the move, fleeing the
collapse of post-World War II materialism in search of a
rebirth of spirit and meaning. The romance of island living is a powerful magnet that seems to live in the
consciousness of everyone pushed to the brink by a tech-
notopian madness that has redefined the yardsticks for
success and contentment to be the gathering of stuff.
They're here in Molokai, on this road. The used car king
from Southern California, who left it all to buy the local
eight-page weekly newspaper; the mini-mall developer
growing white ginger in his tiny hothouse; the chemical
researcher from Croton, Connecticut, now running a
dusty old general store; the sports shoe manufacturer doing nothing in a pole house by the sea, and now . . . me.

All refugees of the soul, fleeing disillusionment and
the horrible ugliness of comfortable neglect. We don't

know why the traditional order of things changed so drastically, but, deep down, there is a confraternity based on guilt that we all allowed ourselves to be seduced into submission by becoming overdependent on so many convenient, but nonessential, things. And now we must reject them or become one of them.

So we run . . . past the city limits into the greenbelts, but soon the sins of the city follow us there, too. We run further still across borders and oceans in the pleasant delusion we have finally outdistanced the certain harvest of endings. The end of more and more of the same as before. The end of plenty. The end of a grand era of secure dreaming.

Uh oh, I'm thinking. Sorry, Mahatma.

Owww! I did it. I sat down. What's wrong with me? Must be the onset of Alzheimer's. Got to walk it off. Boy, that smarts.

Suddenly, I'm in front of yesterday—the most old-fashioned of all Molokai's old-fashioned structures . . . the venerable Ah Ping Store.

It's 1901 again.

Molokai is going through another of its certain cyclical economic tragedies. This time the sugar crop has failed. A previous population of 8,700 shrinks to 1,300. Everyone is leaving to find work on Oahu and the Big Island. Joseph Ah Ping, a quiet, mild-mannered Chinese immigrant cane field worker from Lahaina, Maui, looks across the windswept Kaiwi Channel to the devastated neighbor island and sees nothing but hope and the possibility of realizing his dream—to be a shopkeeper. He comes. He buys four acres on the side of the road in the lush east end. He builds four simple, sturdy, plantation-

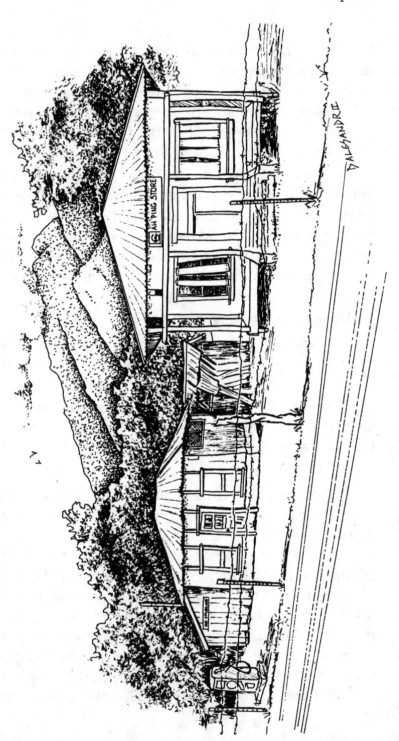

style buildings, all with shiny red tin roofs, bright green exteriors, and well-scrubbed linseed-oiled floors. The tiny shack out back is for mixing poi, the staple of the Hawaiian diet. The next smallest shack will be used for storage and placed out front near the largest building, the general store. He builds a "long house" a few feet from the store for the family sure to come.

They do. Three sons, Ah Ing, Ah Hung, and Ling Wah, and two daughters who always answered to their Western names, Lillian and Katherine. They all pitch in. Mama Ah Ping spends most of her time outdoors, meticulously picking weeds, removing bushelfuls of fallen leaves and ripened mangoes that miraculously seem in constant production.

Mama always pauses in front of her pride and joy, the bougainvillea-rimmed gate, to carefully trim the long, spidery vines that weave their way around the white picket fence. In the middle of a sale, if Mama sees a single leaf fall on the front lawn, she will politely excuse herself to go pick it up. Things must be clean and neat for the customers.

"It's the way we do things, children," Papa says in a voice that rarely rises above a whisper. "Our customers are neighbors. Be kind. Always be kind."

Soon the Ah Ping Store becomes much more than a halfway stop for locals traveling the narrow, oftentimes treacherous country road, where one miscalculation would put you in the ocean on one side or the big rocky ditch on the other. It becomes a gathering place, a haven, a warm campfire at the end of a day of backbreaking work in the fields. A place to "talk story" (Hawaiian expression, meaning to gossip, exchange news, tell tall tales),

laugh, sing, buy some Nehi soda pop, a week-old mainland newspaper, or just look up at a geometric miracle—a
magnificent hanging garden of tin, wood, iron, steel, and
porcelain shapes clustered in a confoundingly tight but
orderly congestion. The ceiling had disappeared, as dripping from every open space on the beams and trusses
were the essentials of island survival: scythes, hoes,
rakes, washboards, fishing rods, toilet seats, rocking
chairs, and a seemingly infinite array of tin boxes and
containers of every size and shape, each with its own very
distinctive label.

Homer Kamalu, the 400-pound stevedore who routinely astonished his fellow workers every day by lifting
130-pound crates by hand at the Pukoo pier, came every
night at seven just to look at the colorful labels in the
hanging gallery and read them out loud. "North Dakota
Screaming Eagle Pine Tar, Wopahachee North Country
Fertilizer, Haywood's Rectal Ointment—The Salve That
Saved the West. Each label got one big pitcha and a whole
history of da place. We did dent have no movie house, so
next best ting to seeing a motion pitcha, huh?"

And, standing in steel-banded barrels next to the
floor-to-ceiling stacks of Spam, Portuguese sausages, and
pork and beans was the store's most demanded item, the
reason every keiki (child) on the island relished a trip to
Ah Ping's—crack seed candy imported from Shanghai,
China.

"You have no money? No worry. Mister Ah Ping will
jest put yur name in da book, if he can remember. You pay
next mont, first ting." Next month rarely came, but Papa
Ah Ping didn't mind. He understood all his neighbor/cus-
tomers were well below the poverty line and worked just
as hard as he did to provide for their families. For years,

very little money changed hands. You need five gallons of kerosene, okay, bring Mr. Ah Ping two fresh squid or sharpen his knives, or bring whatever you can. Barter was the economy, and the Ah Ping Store was where it took place.

When Henry Ford sold some of his new Model A's to the rich pineapple planters on Molokai, the old shopkeeper quickly responded with a single gas pump in front of the tiny shack on the side of the store. If you needed gas after hours, you just knocked on Mr. Ah Ping's house a few feet away. "He geeve you da key, tell you to pump what you need, and pay him first ting next mont. Den he go back to sleep."

When the liquor bars opened on the island in the late thirties and the partying lasted till 3:00, 4:00 in the morning, guilt-ridden revelers filled to the gills with okolehao[1] would whisper below his bedroom window, "Mistah Ah Ping, I forgot to buy some food fo' breakfast. Ma wife gonna keel me. Can you help?" Out he'd come in his nightshirt, holding his big yellow lantern to open the store and square their consciences. Again, never a harsh word. Never a judgment. And so it went for sixty-five years. Through three wars, a Depression, and one agricultural failure after another—cattle, coffee, copra, corn, goats, honey (Molokai was once the world's largest producer of honey), oranges, potatoes, sugar, taro, and wheat. There was always the Ah Ping General Store and the sure hope you could barter dis fo' dat and survive.

In 1965, at the age of ninety, Joseph Ah Ping, suffering from a variety of ailments that prevented him from

---

1   A gin made from rice or pineapple juice

standing tall behind the old hand-cranked cash register and serving his customers, sold the store. But things were just not the same without the original proprietors around. The store closed for good soon thereafter.

The doors haven't been open for twenty-four years, but the four original buildings are still standing proudly, weathered, bent, and rotted through in spots, but erect nevertheless with the tattered, threadbare elegance of the oldest veteran marching in the Fourth of July parade. He knows his time is over, but he will not go meekly. He knows his history deserves one last salute.

The ancient Hawaiians believed all things in the universe—stars, ocean, trees, fish, and rocks—have souls, a life force within that allows them to interact with the flow of nature. Surely, the old Ah Ping Store has a soul. You can feel it every time an occasional tourist slows down when he passes in response to some mystical reverence that sends a message that something really important happened here a long time ago. A soul forged in the dusty red dirt of Molokai at the turn of the century when Filipino, Japanese, Chinese, and Portuguese immigrants risked everything to come to a far-off tiny island to work in the fields and start dreaming of better days. They worked side by side, learned one another's languages, ate one another's foods, sang one another's songs, and lifted one another whenever they fell. It was democracy's finest hour. It will never be found in a history book. But it did happen.

Back to the present.

I'm sitting on the seaside shoulder of the road opposite the store, nursing my wound and admiring the most stunningly apparent feature in all this gentle fading charm—the one thing that seems to strengthen the earth beneath the buildings and buoy their will to keep on fighting the inevitable victory of time and salt air erosion—the grounds are immaculate. Lawn cut uniformly, hibiscus hedges trimmed in exact symmetry, not even the usually ubiquitous dandelion or chickweed in sight, and *not one leaf* on the ground. Considering the 80-by-100-foot lot is ringed with ancient mango trees, the undisputed king of leaf shedders, this phenomenon takes on mystical proportions.

At 10:00 a.m., exactly, the mystery takes on a very simple, human explanation. The door to the "long house" opens and Miss Katherine Ah Ping, age eighty-nine, stands to her full four-foot, ten-inch height, straightens her faded straw sunbonnet, and secures it on her head with a long blue cloth. She wears a long-sleeved, red-checkered work shirt, the kind you see in old photos of California gold rush miners, wrinkled but clean denim overalls, rubber boots, and a sturdy pair of dirt-stained brown-and-white garden gloves. Her movements are an orchestrated ballet in slow motion. First the leaves. Pick them up, take them to the back, and burn them in a large, rusty pot. Down on her hands and knees to pick a few maverick weeds, invisible to the eye at my distance, and then large scissors to trim the grass border around all the buildings. A few minutes' rest on the crumbling concrete steps in front of the store. She pats the top stair, perhaps retrieving a single moment from her childhood memory, and back to work. To the antique, hand-cranked Chevron gas pump in front of the storage shed. Peel the rust slivers away from the hose handle and carefully put them in her large plastic garbage bag. She cleans the glass window on the face of the pump. The frozen numbers read: 49 cents a gallon. Past the sign: Please turn off motor and no smoking please, to the large Drink Coca Cola sign over the store entrance immediately next to the larger Pepsi Cola sign announcing: Ah Ping Store. She adjusts her garden hose to a light spray and points it toward the signs, gently washing off the accumulated red dust. A leaf falls, and she begins her dutiful pantomine all over again.

Miss Katherine has been performing this ritual for twenty-four years, ever since retiring from forty years of elementary school teaching on the island. She never married and continued living in the house where she was born because, as she later told me, "I promised Mama and Papa I would keep the place clean. It was very important to them our store should not become a shame to the community."

I pedaled the Astin Martin down to the Ah Ping Store at the thirteen-mile marker every Tuesday and Saturday, timed to arrive at just about the same time Miss Katherine finished her daily outside chores.

We'd talk at the bougainvillea gate about the mango harvest, the wind, the necessity to take frequent breaks when working in the afternoon sun, the health benefits of napping—you know, the important stuff. Frequently, when a leaf would fall, she would politely excuse herself and go pick it up. Then one Tuesday Miss Katherine wasn't there. Grady, the handyman/beekeeper from Kentucky with the slow Southern drawl and a mouthful of Red Devil chewing tobacco, was there with a small army of cutting, trimming, blowing, and mulching machines.

"Miss Katherine broke her hip. Had to go back to Honolulu. Too old for this work. 'Spect she'll never see

Molokai again." Mr. Grady pauses after every second sentence to spit downwind. "Made me promise to keep the place neat and clean. Funny, this old store hasn't been open in twenty years, but she still had to keep it up. Don't know why. Heard tell the grandkids are just waiting to sell the place for a million-and-a-half dollars." He rubs his big, callused palms across the top of his worn blue denim railroad overalls. "One of those rich people from the mainland running away from the big city will buy it and put up one of those ol' ugly houses." He spits. "They'll never know about the history of this place . . . or care. Well, I suppose people are always looking for a piece of paradise, you know what I mean?"

I know.

We stand in silence for a very long time. A few leaves fall off to the right. I go and pick them up. Mr. Grady smiles.

5

If She Can Sing Every Song of the '40s, It Must Be Love . . . So Much for Solitude

Back at the fairy tale Hoolehua airport. Alone, except for that same sleepy baggage handler and a Goliath-size counter agent delicately picking out chords on his ukulele.

I'm waiting for love. Hannah Marie from Haiku, Maui, arrives in twenty minutes.

I had fully intended to spend my tropical hermitage experience alone, but I distinctly heard one of those little deep down voices say, "Share this contentment with Hannah." I'm relatively certain it came from the heart and not the loins, but I haven't really mastered the art of pinpointing the exact location of "little voices."

Upper-middle-age bachelorhood hath loosed a terrible beast within me, guerrilla love—hit-and-run sex. I resent it and yet knowingly entertain it. I'm not sure if I'm just another weak-willed casualty of our flighty permissive times, or perhaps just sailing through some fifty-plus passage that ominously allows me to see that well-known light at the end of the proverbial tunnel. A frightening light that fraudulently invites all aging men to conquer as many females as possible as proof positive of their immortality.

I think I'm trying to end that charade by genuinely getting closer to the very extraordinary lady about to arrive on the single-engine five-seater Air Molokai flight 107.

Jack London introduced Hannah to me. She was sitting at her desk between a Japanese woodblock print of a rainstorm in Nagoya and a giant ceramic fish. She worked in the art gallery of a hotel at which I was lecturing. I visit galleries about as often as I rotate the tires on my car. Why tonight? Another one of those little voices, I think.

It wasn't love at first sight. No, it was something else—mutual curiosity, I think.

We danced around a bit with small talk, even though the animal inside instantly knew we would become lovers. Funny how we manipulate every other rule of society to serve our selfish ends but steadfastly honor the take-it-one-step-at-a-time mating code of the tribe.

We skipped a few steps when I noticed her reading from my literary hero and spiritual super-ego, Jack London.

"What piece you reading?" I asked.

She cautiously raised her aquamarine eyes over the tops of her fawn-colored bifocals and answered, " 'White Silence,' a short story of being snowed in on the Yukon trail. Ever read it?"

Much to the surprise of the tweedy lookee-loos around us, I leaped between the Remington bronze End of the Trail and the pre-Columbian busts and recited what many literati recognize as the most beautifully descriptive paragraph ever written:

"The afternoon wore on, and with the awe, born of the White Silence, the voiceless travelers bent to their work. Nature has many tricks wherewith she convinces man of his finity—the ceaseless flow of the tides, the fury of the storm, the shock of the earthquake, the long roll of heaven's artillery— but the tremendous, the most stupefying of all, is the passive phase of the White Silence. All movement ceases, the sky clears, the heavens are as brass, the slightest whisper seems sacrilege, and man becomes timid, affrighted at the sound of his own voice. Sole speck of life journeying across the ghostly wastes of a dead world, he trembles at his audacity, realizes that his is a maggot's life, nothing more. Strange thoughts arise unsummoned, and the mystery of all things strives for utterance. And the fear of death, of God, of the universe, comes over him—the hope of the Resurrection and the Life, the yearning for immortality, the vain striving of the imprisoned essence. . . ."

We say the final line together as if on cue.

". . .it is then, if ever, man walks alone with God."

Hannah, the classic, self-contained Libra, was flushed with embarrassment. It wouldn't be the last time my

If She Can Sing Every Song of the '40s, It
Must Be Love . . .

39

impromptu outbursts would redden her cheeks. Two Japanese tourists ask for my autograph. One of the tweedies intones, "You sure know your Bible, young man." Hannah melts down behind her counter.

We met later that night at the encased display of the shark's jaw in the lobby. We agreed to have a mini-picnic on the rocky cliffs encircling the hotel grounds. I brought grapes, apples, orange slices, low-cal cheese, and spring water. Something told me she was a "health food only" child of the earth. She was, and a whole lot more. Retired child psychologist, former barnstorming pilot, world traveler, hiker, defender of the planet, expert on North American wildflowers, and the possessor of the most colorful eclectic art collection on the island of Maui. None of which bonded us until I discovered what, to me, was her most seductive talent—she loved songs of the forties!

For two days we sang every one of them. When I found she was the only other person in North America, besides me, who knew all the words to Bing Crosby's classic "I Only Want a Buddy Not A Sweetheart," love bloomed.

It was consummated three months later on a return trip. We jitterbugged to my "Best of the '40s" for two hours on her antique Oriental rug ringed by priceless East Indian mosaics, eighteenth-century Hawaiian poi pounders, Balinese fertility masks, and a smiling array of Hopalong Cassidy artifacts. We then lay down on her Iranian scatter rug beneath her four-foot golden Buddha and grabbed a measure of immortality. We became, most likely, the first couple to make love to the accompaniment of the crashing, burping, belching musical madness of Spike Jones' "You Always Hurt The One You Love." We just didn't have the hormonal control to wait for "As Time Goes By."

Maui Hannah arrives. A blond, forty-something Katherine Hepburn. Strong, athletic, nonconforming, independent free spirit, with a copy of *Mother Earth News* tucked under one well-muscled arm and a Sierra Club knapsack slung over the other.

Her cheeks start to redden as she gets closer and reads the sign I'm holding up over my head: "Congratulations Henry/Hannah. Your Sex Change Looks Great!"

6

I Think I've Finally Solved the Problem of Male/ Female Relationships

An old man with mustard stains on his shirt and a compulsion to burp after every sentence taught me the penultimate lesson on successful relationships. He and two X-rated dudes named Kempton and Wace.

Dr. Eric was eighty, retired from the chairmanship of the psychology department of a large Ivy League university, and a much ballyhooed author and lecturer on why boys and girls have so much trouble living with one another. A raspy curmudgeon who never was in favor with his gold cufflinked peers, he survived because every orthodoxy needs its eccentrics to deflate its pomposity and liven up its cocktail parties. A little nearby heresy somehow intensifies the belief of the faithful.

Several years ago, I was the after-dinner speaker for that same faithful, gathered in a $500-a-night hotel-palace by a man-made lake in Dallas to hear the latest "How To" millionaire authors offer their pop wisdom on why the male/female relationship was falling apart in modern times. They invited Dr. Eric along as an afterthought. Psychiatrists, psychologists, marriage counselors, and starry-eyed sociology majors leaned forward in their seats, clicked on their cassette recorders, and drank in every syllable of pap that came oozing from the well-scrubbed mouths of the gods. TV cameras zoomed in, and Buck Rogers technology sent their pictures to millions more around the world. Mount Olympus had been reduced to twenty-five inches.

On and on they droned about nuclear family, pleasure replacing value, asynchronous sexual behavior, Dostoyevsky, premature ejaculation as the norm, Jung, Freud, Madonna, penis envy and the corporate female, and a very detailed description of the elasticity of the vagina complete with a thirty-foot overhead projected slide of the delicate subject matter. Not the sort of thing to rivet your attention, particularly right after a lunch of crab Louie and chocolate mousse.

The compulsory question-and-answer routine followed, with more doublespeak and vapid grammar. Lots of definitions and no solutions. Finally, a stern-faced lady in a tailored auburn suit and bejeweled tinted glasses addressed the panel, "We'd like to wrap things up with your practical suggestions on how to restore health and commitment to relationships."

The majority of answers bunched around stuff like, "spiritual renewal," "restructuring the community," "compulsory term marriages" and "isolating the bonding gene."

Ms. Auburn now reluctantly turns to the old man with the mustard stains on his shirt. She had deftly

avoided him until now. Probably because of his total con-
centration on blowing large, thick smoke rings with his
long, fat, asymmetrical cigar. That and his occasional volcanic belching spree.

She lets out an audible sigh and asks, "Dr. Eric, surely
you must have an opinion on why male-female relationships are falling apart in America."

The old man smiles and blows his largest ring so far.
"I surely do."

A long pause in which the crusty old doctor belches
twice, blows his nose, and drops a half ton of ash from his
cigar onto his wrinkled blue jacket. The cameras zoom in
for a close-up of the rumpled senior distinguished panel
member.

The faithful lean forward just a little more.

He offers his wisdom, "I've been married fifty-seven
years to the same woman, written forty-three books on
relationships, and counseled thousands of couples in
pain, and here's what I've learned . . . men usually marry
the woman that gives them the biggest hard-on, plain
and simple."

After a collective gasp of horror from the charcoal gray
audience, Auburn Lady's pencil-thin lips go into mini-con-
vulsions. She drops her legal size notepad and clicks off
several "tsk, tsks." Dr. Mustard Stain takes another long
puff of his cigar and continues. "It's a good reason to mate,
but not to marry. I believe we have to educate every male
and female at a very young age to distinguish between lust
and love. To demystify marriage and lay it bare as a social
and legal contract to mutually provide some physical and
humanistic services. It should be a mandatory course for
every child who reaches puberty. Stop the geometry, the

hula lessons, and the driver's ed, and drum into their heads the sensible criteria needed to make the biggest decision of their lives."

The indignation is quickly turning to nods of agreement and genuine listening.

Dr. Eric leans back in his chair revealing yet another flaw in his personal grooming—a fly at half mast. This one he notices and nonchalantly reaches down and corrects the problem in front of eighteen hundred live folks and another four million or so watching their teleconferencing screens in classrooms and auditoriums around the world.

"There are no $100-an-hour shrinks, gurus, or bestselling authors who can tell you how to select the right mate, but I'll tell you this—I absolutely do know two things should be present for the possibility of a successful relationship. One, marry or associate with someone of a complementary temperament as you. When you talk, does the other person listen? Does he/she honor the silence, or are they always interrupting? Do your dispositions balance or conflict? Two, marry or associate with someone as positive as you or more positive than you. A negative person always, always brings down the positive one in a relationship. In my experience, every other piece of knowledge regarding relationships is a lot of crapola."

I'm thinking about old Dr. Mustard Stain's saucy wisdom as I watch Maui Hannah balled up in the wicker chair on the lanai. She's reading Charmian London's *A Diary of the Cruise of the Snark*, a fascinating, detailed account of the adventurous London's bully trip around the Pacific in a leaking forty-five-foot sailboat in 1907. I'm sitting on the bed in the next room reading husband Jack's infamous treatise on the fallacy of romance as the glue for relationships,

The Kempton-Wace Letters.[1] It is no less adventurous (for its time), principally for its frank assessment of America's mating habits.

We sit quietly for hours, each absorbed in his and her lifelong fascination with the Londons' zest for discovery, play, and childlike reverence for the sparkle and shine of untouched nature.

Two lone riders, together but apart, testing the uncertain and unfamiliar waters of intimacy. Will the new calm of my treehouse experience finally bring me a lifelong mate?

Every so often we shout out an interesting tidbit to the other.

I go first. "Listen to this, Hannah. Dane Kempton writes to his friend Herbert Wace telling him he's met the most magnificent lady, and he intends to marry her posthaste. He says he's found true romantic love that 'I feel myself in sight of my portion of immortality on earth.' The practical Wace writes back, that 'romance is temporary insanity . . . a blind mating of the blind, a suspension of reason that blocks out the more critical non-sex matters.' "

She smiles and hops right back aboard the *Snark*. Hours pass unnoticed like the subtle shift of an evening tide. We honor one another's silence.

As a burning sunset changes the color scheme of the Pacific from sky blue to autumn orange, I get in the last literary flash. "Here it is, Hannah, the phrase that got Jack's book yanked from the shelves by prudish librarians all over the country. Wace tells Kempton the 'only

---

1   Published by MacMillan Company, 1903

true foundation for a lasting relationship is . . . sex comradeship, friends who have fun loving. On that affection,' he says, 'you can build everything substantial two people need to endure and grow.' Whatdaya think?"

She doesn't respond. Instead, she gets up and walks into the bathroom. A few minutes later she emerges wearing a camouflage-colored shorty nightgown, khaki underwear, sneakers, and a Groucho Marx mustache. She takes out her well-oiled baseball mitt and a heavily abused softball, tosses it in the air, and asks, "Wanna catch?"

I do. We toast the end of another simple miracle, a day on Molokai, with a vigorous game of catch on the front lawn.

She backhands the hard grounders and snares the line drives with flawless dexterity. I flub two grounders and drop a pop fly.

She jogs over, kisses my cheek, pats my fanny, and offers me a way out: "Pretty tough playing into the sun, eh?"

The sun has been asleep in the horizon for half an hour.

Sex comradeship.

Hannah leaves two days later. Three weeks after that, a letter arrives at my Star Route 324 mailbox. It's from Hannah. She's met an American history professor from Princeton, New Jersey. She's convinced he's the mate fate had her created for, so she's moving in with him back East.

"I loved our fun together but realized you really did only want a buddy, not a sweetheart."

Perhaps, perhaps.

7

A Streetcar Named Delirious

On Mondays and Wednesdays I ride the "Streetcar Named Delirious."

That's what Aunty Tunee calls it. The state calls it the Maui Economic Opportunity Bus, picking up and delivering Molokai's senior citizens to the Mitchell Pauole social center for a hot meal, blood pressure check, and a group sing-along.

Molokai's a friendly place willing to bend a rule or two if it will help somebody get through the day. So Kane (pronounced "Kar-nay"), the no-neck driver with the body of the Incredible Hulk and a Charlie Chan mustache, drives six miles out of his way to pick up me and my laundry and deposit us in the middle of town. If I can complete my wash cycle before the six regular riders finish their soup and song, I get a ride back. I never miss an opportunity to be with the youngest old people I have ever known.

What a gang.

There's Aunty Tunee, 89, who routinely turns every calamity into a carefree day at Disneyland. Once during a torrential downpour that washed away bridges, cows, and a two-story warehouse and threatened to sweep our little bus off the coastal road into the angry Pacific, she cheerfully remarked, "At least it's a clean rain. Don't forget to enjoy it." No one quite understood what that meant, but somehow we were reassured. And she gave all her ailments names and frequently talked to them. Her arthritis was Momi (pearl); her two bleeding ulcers were Amoko (Amos) and Analu (Andy); her high blood pressure was Akaka (Agatha); her stomach cancer was Ipo (sweetheart). She reasoned, "If you give your troubles friendly names, they can't hurt you, you know what I mean, young man?"

Yes, Aunty Tunee, I know.

Then there were the diminutive, stringbean-thin Japanese sisters Fumi and Masako, 90-plus, retired pineapple field workers who wore matching chartreuse backpacks, Grateful Dead T-shirts, and U.S. Keds sneakers, the high-top kind. They had nothing in their packs but dreams. They would talk about imagined hiking trips they were going to make. Tuesday they were going to trek through the soft and frequently treacherous sand of Mo'omomi Dunes. The fact that some of the world's heartiest outdoorsmen had given up the challenge didn't bother them at all. "We're gonna take small steps and rest in da shade." On Friday they were going to descend 3,000 feet down the narrow rocky switchback trail at Kukuiohapu'u to the leper colony at Kalaupapa. Never mind Klondike muleskinners would shiver in their chaps at the thought. The ladies had a foolproof plan. "We take along plenty cornstarch to keep our feet fresh and dry. No problem."

Aunty Malia, 94, admired Shirley Temple and had the curly blond wig, sailor suit dress, and patent leather shoes to prove it. Her kewpie doll makeup with the blotchy rouged cheeks, orange lips, and crooked eyelashes were, I'm sure, her projection of Shirley in her golden years. She was a brazen hussy and made no pretense of hiding it. She had been lobbying unsuccessfully for six years to include "touch dancing" in the senior citizen lunch program. The state told her they can't get liability insurance to cover it.

Francisco, 83, spent seventy years as a paniolo (cowboy), herding cattle for the rich missionary families of the island. Now he spends his time decorating his walker with fresh flowers every day, sewing patches on everything he wears, and recommending long-life remedies. His latest—drink a little iodine in water every day to improve your circulation.

Finally, there's Doc Chu, 86, once the most feared man on Molokai. Hard to believe just the mere mention of this neatly dressed, placid little man in the bottle-bottom glasses would turn brave hearts to Jell-O. For over forty years, Doc Chu was the only dentist on the island. Kane, the no-neck driver, apparently spoke for every set of teeth on the island when he told me, "He nevah use no needle or gas when he drill or pull yur teet. Jest put his knee on yer chest and yank. Oh boy, you could hear da screams all the way down the street. Even da min-is-tah at church use to tell us to pray so we no get any cavities. I tink everybody in dose days were so frightened we used to brush our teet six or seven times a day."

Now the Doc reads every story in his *Reader's Digest* and kindly offers it to anybody who "wants to read about how to make life simple." I once asked him why he smiled all the time. He said, "It relieves the discomfort in my mouth. My false teet don't fit so gud." His smile turned to a deep, good-natured laugh and he added, "Poetic justice, eh!" More laughter.

The "Streetcar Named Delirious" was filled with veteran practitioners of life who never saw obstacles, only ways around, over, or under the roadblocks. They smiled a lot, laughed at most everything, and always seemed to be looking for new things.

Growing old brings a lot of pain and discomfort. No amount of positive thinking can erase that reality, but, as Aunty Tunee says, "It's like every ting else, it's how you play wit it dat counts."

In a few weeks this hearty bunch of seniors will provide me with the most improbable, hilarious but stunningly beautiful example that you're never too old to seize the moments of your day and create magic. Later.

8

Searching for Elephants with the "Witch Hazel Man"

When he occasionally rode the "Streetcar Named Delirious," the haole[1] man always sat in the back, apart from the predictable chatter and routine rituals. He wore the same clothes day in and day out—a faded aloha shirt with birds of paradise in graceful flight, baggy blue trousers, white socks, and leather moccasins. Always neat, well groomed, content. His only extravagance was an overabundant use of witch hazel as his after-shave lotion. Its cool, antiseptic odor was a favorite of all the riders. The wheezy sounds of inhalation turned up a notch whenever he boarded the yellow-and-black bus on the edge of the banana grove at the thirteen-mile marker.

My guess was that he was in his late seventies. You couldn't tell that from his lean, muscle-taut body and cat-like moves, but the hands never lie. They were in their late seventies for sure. He was a pleasant man with a soft,

---

1   White person; foreigner, non-Hawaiian

easy smile, but he never talked. He acknowledged every greeting with a friendly grin, no more. He just sat in the back, taking in the scenery and then quickly jotting down notes in an old brown covered notebook with a thick lead pencil, the kind butchers and carpenters used in the old days.

He was a poet and songwriter, frequently composing in the back of his book and then reciting or humming his creations under his breath, quietly, and just indistinguishable enough to leave you guessing as to the quality of the work.

When the composing and notetaking was over, he'd dip into a battered leather satchel and retrieve a book, always overflowing with dozens of multicolored tabs of every description— brown paper, feathers, leaves, toothpicks, dental floss, bits of newspaper, anything handy was pressed into service as a marker whenever he discovered a worthy thought.

And what books. After several trips I became quite proficient at getting as close as possible to him without disturbing his strict territorial imperative. Bending, twisting, and sneaking a peek, I read such titles as: *The Politics of Extinction; The Cambridge Medieval History, Volume II; The Rise of the Saracens; A History of Sexuality in America;* and *The Audubon Society Handbook for Butterfly Watchers.* There was no limit to his range of inquiry. This was no ordinary resigned septuagenarian on his way to his daily state-sponsored free lunch and singalong. I had a feeling I could learn something from him.

I tried everything to engage him in conversation. Nothing. Just a slight smile and a closed door.

On one occasion I even bathed myself in a quarter bottle of witch hazel before boarding the bus. Who knows, maybe like odors attract. They don't. The only reaction I got came from Aunty Tunee, "How come you stink so much today?"

I've always been fascinated by the elderly. I think it's more primordial than romantic. They're at where we're all going, and the human animal is always obsessed by journey's end. Well, in everything but aging. We seem to work very hard at avoiding that final inquiry with the same passionate denegration we show toward death.

Maybe it's my Roman heritage, "All we seek has been written in history," Caesar's Gallic wars, or was it Marcello Mastrioani in *La Dulce Vita*? Or maybe I'm just as bone-scared as the next fleshy mortal and figure by studying old people I'll never become one. Could be the same Puritan prevention logic that seduced me when I was an eight-year-old altar boy. I figured if I acted like a priest, I'd never go to hell. For weeks I went around with the petrified saintly grin of a martyr, patting people on the shoulder and then blessing them. I even carried a Sheffield milk bottle filled with contraband holy water scooped out of the church fountain. When I started hearing the confessions of little girls in the second grade, my teacher, Sister Mary Olivia, sent me to the school nurse for counseling. It worked. She was young, pretty, and the only female in 1946 to wear short, short skirts. When she sat down they inched dangerously close to being a mortal sin. I lost my vocation instantly.

Back to the haole man on the bus.

I made inquiries. No one knew his name, but everybody knew something about him. Lila, the large, pure-blooded Hawaiian lady who ran the crafts shop called him the "Witch Hazel Man."

"Oh yeah, he comes in every day and puts me trew da terd da-gree," she said with a big hearty laugh.

She explained as she glided around the shop dusting her shiny koa bowl collection, "I can smell him before I can see him coming. Den he pops in, geeves me one beeg 'aloha,' and starts askin' questions."

"What kind of questions?" I ask.

"All kinds about everyting. How dis bowl was carved, how da Hawaiians mix paint to get certain colors, how we weave feathers to make da lei hulas.[2] Dat buggah ask about everyting. Den you know what? He writes everyting down in his book. You tink maybe he gonna write one novel and make me famous like Scarlett O'Hara or somebody." Again, Lila, the happy Hawaiian, lets out a giant roar of laughter, setting off a mini-symphony of tinkling sounds from her hanging crystal mobiles.

Sri, the part-Pakistani, part-Filipino supervisor at the one-room library on the edge of town, confirms the inquisitive behavior of the Witch Hazel Man.

"He takes out more books than anyone else on the island."

"What kind?" I ask.

"All kinds, but mostly 'how-to' stuff. You know, how to build this, how to be a better that, how to survive in the wilderness. . ." She pauses and then asks, "How come you're asking all these questions?"

---

2   Feathered headbands for hats

"I think I'm trying to stay young."

She stifles a modest laugh with her index finger.

The beat goes on. Bobo, the rotund proprietor and resident philosopher of the oldest gas station in town, brightens at the sound of the Witch Hazel Man.

"I call him every time I have a beeg repair job and he comes over to watch."

"Howcum?"

"He said he jest likes to know how to do tings."

This one saw him gathering nuts, hiking through the hills of Mauna Olu'olu on the east end. That one saw him studying stones at the ancient adze quarry at Kanewai on the west end. Every story a tale of motion, going, coming, doing. Never a stand-still-and-just-look story.

Kane, the no-neck bus driver, lets me off at the east end of the banana grove. He points through the shadows of the thick growth of wide, flapping banana leaves and maverick vines.

"About a quarter mile trew dere you come to a little shack wit a tin roof. Dat's him."

There was a problem with his directions.

"Wait a minute, Kane, there's no road here. How am I going to find his house?"

"Follow da smell." His belly laugh overpowered the screeching of his two-wheel U-turn as he jetted off toward Kaunakakai.

There was no path, but there was a way. Zigzagging through dense elephant grass, past mud flats, the keawe thickets, and the tons of hard green bananas bunched close enough to form a near impenetrable natural fortress, I came upon a tin-roofed shack in a clearing. Except for the outhouse, it was something you might expect in a Grimm's fairy tale. It was ringed with a dozen varieties of colorful flowers, symmetrically planted and meticulously maintained. At one end was a neatly trimmed grove of fruit trees, lilikoi, breadfruit, tangerine, and lemon. At the other end was a very elaborate and comprehensive vegetable garden of more varieties than I could identify. Several handmade birdhouses were being put to good use by a flock of chatty residents. There were no signs of modern conveniences. No overhead wires, no TV antennae, no car, no outside lighting. The water catchment system, the outdoor plumbing, and the squeaky sound of a water pump from inside all confirmed the Witch Hazel Man was fully self-sufficient.

I walked under the hibiscus-covered trellis at the front of the house and knocked at the door.

But what do I say? "Hi, I'm a nosy fifty-year-old in some kind of post-mid-life transition, just hanging out in nature waiting for the clouds to part and hear a *vox Dei* to give me enough hope to want to push ahead to sixty. In the meantime, I bother as many old people as possible looking for—I don't know what the hell. Are you having a nice day?"

He opened the door. I opted for simplicity.

"Howdy. I brought you some oranges." I handed him a brown paper bag filled with six Friendly Market oranges.

His eyes widened and his head tilted forward and to the left, clearly indicating the three robust trees at the side of the house gushing with hundreds of the biggest, ripest, healthiest oranges imaginable. He looked back at me with that same look I get from the inspector at my tax

audit every time I tell him I have over seven thousand dollars in charitable deductions.

I filled the next several silent awkward moments look-ing around his large one-room sanctuary in hope of filling in more of the puzzle of the Witch Hazel Man. His sur-roundings spoke volumes. All handmade furniture cut with designer accuracy from the available supply sur-rounding the house—bamboo, keawe, pine, and sandalwood. Original watercolors of island landscapes covered the walls, along with shelves of books, piles of books, and clusters of books. An artist's easel with a half-completed painting of the sacred Moa'ula Falls sat in one corner and in the other, past dozens of hand-carved Ha-waiian figurines and lauhala baskets, sat a small weaver's loom with the embryonic stages of something in its intricate webbing. And in the center of the organized clutter, supported by two freshly cut logs, was an old Chevy engine block. Alongside it lay a half-open book, *How To Repair Your Own Car.*

Over the small homemade pine bed was an aging, water-stained poster photo of a man obviously fated to open many doors for me, none other than Jack London, caught in a contemplative moment, jotting down some notes on the deck of his beloved *Snark.* The quotation under the picture was obliterated by time and the ele-ments. I instinctively filled them in . . . out loud:

"I would rather be a superb meteor, every atom of me in magnificent glow, than a sleepy and permanent planet. The proper function of man is to live, not to exist. I shall not waste my days in trying to prolong them. I shall use my time."

My reluctant host instantly lost his suspicion, beamed ear to ear with a boyish grin of discovery, and spoke, "You know London?"

"He's a very dear, personal friend," I replied. From that moment the Witch Hazel Man of Molokai and I were friends.

In the several weeks that followed, we would talk for hours . . . searching for elephants. I'd better explain.

You see, the Witch Hazel Man had this "thing" about elephants. He believed they were the most magnificent and magical creatures on the face of the earth. That to look one squarely in the eye was the only real adventure left in the world.

"Elephants have been around longer than any other giant in the universe. They know the secret to survival. That's real magic." The obvious fact that there wasn't an elephant within 2,500 miles of Molokai didn't faze him one bit. So off we went almost every day . . . searching for elephants. To the Weloku Heiau,[3] to the Moanui Sugar Mill ruins, in a dugout canoe to Moku Ho'oniki Island, nesting place for hundreds of exotic seabirds a few miles off the breezy eastern tip of Molokai. We never brought food or water. No need. My affable companion had learned the ways of the woods. He'd studied everything Euell Gibbons[4] had ever written. He knew what fruit and nuts to pluck from the trail and eat with confidence. He knew where mountain streams produced the purest water and where to find shelter during the sudden rain squalls that blew in off the Pacific. He knew the tides and

---

3   Ancient Hawaiian temple of worship
4   Author and expert on edible plants

always felt the subtle shift of the tradewinds. He taught me many useful things to know in nature—the rarity of blue flowers, which coconut to pick for the softest inside meat (stay away from the lowest hanging one; go for the one closest to the shoot of the tree), how to survive a fall into quicksand (roll over on your back to increase the surface mass of your body), the rascal qualities of the magpie birds who find great delight deceiving all around them by imitating the sounds of other birds, the easiest way to identify dangerous plants. The latter is especially significant information for a city kid who once flunked his Boy Scout wildlife merit badge by identifying poison sumac as an edible fern and then proceeding to gleefully cook a half pound of the lethal greenery for his trail supper. We covered every wilderness area on the island, but we never found elephants. But somehow he made me believe it was important to look.

Early one evening, after a long day of searching, we sat on the old wooden steps of Our Lady of Sorrows Church, one of a half dozen built by the leper priest Father Damien in the 1880s. I asked him why he crowded so much learning and doing into one day. He was busy at the time identifying the navigational stars by their Hawaiian names. He gave me the wait-a-minute sign, jotted down some notes in his book, closed it very slowly, held the big stubby pencil up to the side of his nose and said, very matter-of-factly, "Waiting is doing the devil's work."

He pulled out his corncob pipe, homemade, of course, and started packing it with his home-grown blend.

"Old H.L. Mencken was right. 'Aside from the here and now, all other knowledge is bunkum.' All we've got is the here and now, a tiny flick of time. Exalt it the best way you know how—feed your brain with something you didn't know before. Do something to push your sense of discovery. Every problem we have in this world right now can be traced to people doing nothing to make themselves better than they were in the last moment."

He took a few big puffs of his crooked little pipe and smiled.

"You probably wanna know why I don't engage all those folks on the bus in talk, right?"

I nodded yes. He continued.

"Because I don't want to talk about old things, yesterday's stuff. I've learned to ask myself the most important question in the universe. . . ."

I leaned forward. I didn't want to miss this. I had given up climbing mountaintops in Nepal looking for wise old holy men or sequestering myself in a Trappist monastery in southern Spain to come to Molokai to find this next piece of wisdom.

Here it is, "What's the best use of my time right now? Is it complaining about things I can't change, or is it writing a poem, making a note to study some magical thing in nature, or digging a cistern, or planting a philodendron tree. How many prophets do we need?! The secret to a valuable life is out—persistent meaningful effort toward some worthy goal. What other merit have we? You agree?"

I nodded yes.

He puffed and continued.

"I believe you measure that effort one minute at a time. Hell, we're all Minutemen. Do something now! Don't wait on line. Read a book. Jot down an idea. Learn a new word. Something to fill the moment."

His voice dropped down to a whisper.

"I've read every philosophy, every religion, every renowned soothsayer and essayist, and I haven't come across a more practical piece of good living information than that."

We sat there in silence for a mighty long time, just watching a great architect at work. Adding a star here, a constellation there, and constantly rearranging the shapes and movements of a magnificent parade of white linen clouds. It seemed to be the best use of our moments at the time.

I never saw the Witch Hazel Man again. He died four days later. I'd like to report that he expired in a dramatic blaze of meaning, perhaps defending a wounded deer from merciless poachers, or slumped over his homemade pinewood writing desk trying to figure out the ultimate syllogisms of Aquinas, or maybe clinging to a windswept rocky precipice painting a startling expressionist vision of a tropical paradise. He didn't. He died like all poets die, prosaically, far from thunder and glory, wrapped up in small things. He died at his kitchen table, clipping coupons. We buried him in the old Kaunakakai cemetery on the east end of town. The one where relatives and friends leave little gifts they think their recently departed loved ones might enjoy on their eternal journey. You'll find candy bars, bow ties, bowling trophies, a *Police Gazette*, and quite a few false teeth. Now you can add one sixteen-ounce bottle of Dickinson's pure witch hazel and a one-foot-high, hand-carved African bull elephant.

Aloha, my friend.

9

There's Always a Better Way to the Top of the Mountain

John and I are getting closer . . . ten feet, now. What a difference a half-pint of 2% a day makes. Now he follows me everywhere and occasionally says a few words. Today, as I hike up Kamakou, there he is, trailing behind, mumbling under his breath.

A quarter of the way up the rugged face of the leeward side, as I hack through thickets of scrub brush and needle-sharp keawe, searching for a safe passage, he disappears. Aha! Mister Smug is a quitter. I should have known. Can't take it when the going gets tough.

Several hours later, I reach the halfway point, bloodied, slightly torn, and limping on two swollen ankles. I'm in no shape to continue, and I haven't got the will to go back down.

What to do? A new sound. A cat meowing a few yards to the east. At least I think it's a cat. I hobble through the punishing undergrowth and discover it is, indeed, a cat . . . Mister John Muir, sitting pompously in the middle of a clean, clear, soft footpath stretching neatly from the base to the 4,900-foot summit of my heretofore impenetrable tormentor.

"So why didn't you tell me there was a hiking trail, Muir?"

"I did, dummy. But you were too busy flexing your macho to pay attention."

I'm too tired and too sore to argue. I need to rest.

I have every intention of finding some dry leaves and making a bed for the night, but more insult to an already shredded ego appears. Mert and Marge nonchalantly waddle up the trail, exchange a few words with Muir, and start to the top. All three pause and turn back to me with that "Well, are-you-or-aren't-you-coming?" look. What choice does a bowed mortal have in that circumstance? We all reach the top of the world together shortly after noon and sit quietly watching the heavens with that same sense of peaceful awe I'm sure Hillary and Tenzing must have shared the first time atop Mount Everest. The only difference being their silent adoration was never broken by the most mortifying sound in the great outdoors—a totally uncivilized, self-righteous scrubby little cat snickering under his breath.

10

Can a Catholic Voyeur Consummate the Ultimate Sex Fantasy in Front of Seventeen Mud Hens?

Patrella, the TWA Flight 403 Fantasy Lady in Blue, explodes back into my life.

Dressed in a sweaty, well-worn Banana Republic chic safari outfit, she guns her rusting World War II jeep up my front hill and hits the horn. "Ahoy, in the treehouse. Come on down and play!"

A big hug, a fast tour of my rustic hideout, and an invite to join her nature group for their "sunset ceremony."

I pack a toothbrush and some Paco Rabanne Pour Homme cologne and hop in the front seat. She picks some mangoes, wanders into the tall grass, and comes back holding, oh no, John Muir in her arms.

"Isn't he cute. And so friendly, he just came over to me and started nuzzling." I knew it. The little phony is a pervert.

Beat it, Muir. This is my fantasy.

She insists on taking him. He jumps into the back seat. I don't believe it. Lust for the same woman has narrowed our trust gap down to three feet. But it's only temporary, I'm sure. He's sitting back there with that damn catlike smirk that says, "You haven't got a chance, dummy. She's crazy about me."

We drive the eighteen miles on the southern coast road through Kaunakakai on to the Maunaloa Highway up into the mountains and then west twelve miles to Mahana. We turn north, tighten our seat belts, and bump and chug our way through seven miles of a practically impassable, deep-gutted jeep road, arriving at one of Hawaii's greatest natural wonders, Mo'omomi Dunes. Muir jumped out after the first big bump and followed behind.

Mo'omomi is old Hawaii. Real old. Probably before there were footprints in Polynesia there was this 900 acres of majestic "white silence"—rolling, shifting dunes of glistening sand huddled along the shoreline. One of nature's first great soft designs. A Sahara by the sea.

Mo'omomi, a child of the wind, was created by the persistent northeast trades carrying sand inland and then gently dropping it in long, shimmering strips.

I've been at the mouth of the Tigris and Euphrates at sunrise. I've sailed the Ganges in the moonlight. They are indeed mystical places, but my soul never confirmed what scholars only suspect—this is where time began. Here at Mo'omomi the conviction is loud and certain.

All around us is vegetation you have never seen before or will never see again. A half dozen varieties of endangered beach plants are making a last stand against the assault of civilization. Fossil shells of extinct land snails and the petrified remains of rare Hawaiian birds pepper the nearby sandstone rocks.

The list of treasures at Mo'omomi is long. Green sea turtles nest there. So do beautifully patterned ghost crabs. Laysan albatrosses soar above the breaking waves. Ocean naupaka and beach morning glories color the waterline. And everywhere are fading echoes of the songs and chants of ancient Hawaii, accompanied by the never-ending symphony of crashing waves. The Witch Hazel Man used to say this is where God chose to lay down to rest on the seventh day.

Patrella expresses her wonderment in her unique, disjointed English. "Of all the places I've been with our group, this has the most powerful natural vibrations I've ever felt. We have a portable potty on the ridge if you have to go."

I don't. We walk down to the water's edge and meet her group. Seventeen of them. They're upbeat and friendly with those sappy, 1960s peace-and-love-flower-child smiles. They are also jaybird naked! Muir retreats to the ridge behind us and sits quietly beside the outhouse. Patrella quickly disrobes, revealing what every guy on Flight 403 imagined. More voluptuous than athletic, she is every inch of what a fifty-year-old voyeur could hope for. Her large, firm breasts draw applause from three of the flower children. I'd clap, too, but I'm a little confused. I didn't plan on seventeen other naked people in my fantasy.

She's excited, "You can take off your clothes if you want, Treehouse. We all just adopt a single name here. We'll call you Treehouse, okay? I'm Capriccio. Clothing is optional. Come on to the mud pit. We're getting ready for the 'sunset communion' ceremony."

I compromise. I strip to my navy blue boxer shorts. I'm not going to give Muir the satisfaction of seeing my total capitulation to these Fruit Loops. The flower children giggle a lot and are very fond of the word "grand." It's a grand day, a grand place, and isn't friendship in nature a grand experience.

The "sunset communion" is led by a lawyer from Snohomish, Washington, who calls himself "Blueness." He directs everybody to the pit, where they proceed to cover themselves, head to toe, in the oozy red clay of Molokai. I guess every fantasy has a price tag so, whatdahell, I join the clay people.

Blueness explains the ritual. You lie at the water's edge facing the fading sun, stretching your arms and legs as wide apart as possible to give Mother Earth as large a target as possible to fill your body with "the flow of nature."

He adds, "Once you feel the force field vibrations, do what it directs you to do."

For three couples it directs them to "make it" in the surf. Most everyone else is directed to massage someone else's body real slow. Capriccio asks me, "Do you want to make love, Treehouse?" I kinda do, but I can't. Suddenly, my estrangement from all things modern overwhelms me—I am, unmistakenly, a fifty-something guy caught in a thirty-something world I don't recognize or care to. What am I even doing here with these naked dipsticks?

All this plus Sister Mary Petrie of Sacred Heart Grammar School, Glendale, Queens, New York, shouting in my ear, "Robert, what would your mother think? Choose now, young man, heaven or hell." I learn conclusively in this comically ironic moment one of the greatest lessons of middle age—the faith of your youth ultimately overtakes the adult. I should have known better. After all, didn't I feel this same guilt when I was fifteen and stood in the shadows behind the audience at the Hudson Burlesque Theatre in New Jersey? I spent more time scanning the crowd to make sure none of my neighbors were there than I did watching the naughty ladies peeling off their clothes. I just don't have the genetic structure for this kind of thing.

I get up, walk a few hundred yards down the beach, bury my underwear, wash my lustful body clean, and dress.

Muir and I walk the seven miles back to the main road, hitch a ride on the back of a watermelon truck, and arrive home close to midnight. A half-pint of 2% for John and a long hot shower for me.

I guess fantasies do you the most good when they stay where they belong . . . inside, dancing with all the other elusive possibilities.

11

Dammit, God—I Want an Answer Now, and, No, I'm Not Going to Make My Bed

Day seventeen. Early A.M. Can't sleep. Restless night. No syntax, just feelings. Here they are: Who am I kidding? My man-in-the-wilderness bit isn't working . . . nature isn't everything Thoreau said it would be . . . there's no achievement in nature, no reward for ambition, just relentless process . . . carbon dioxide in, oxygen out . . . day into night, life into death, strong eat the weak, indescribable wonder into brutal battles for survival, hot, cold, vapor, rain and back again . . . but I'm not a tree, I'm not a chipmunk, I'm not a reef mollusk, I'm Gemini . . . I'm blood and marrow, spirit and inclination . . . the nature in me needs constant achievement! Dammit, I'm tired of waiting for answers to feed all those funny voices inside beating a tattoo on my self-esteem. Dammit, God! I'm fifty years old. I want my answers now! I'm a good person, I paid my dues, you owe it to me . . . where do I go from here? And I am not going to make

70

my bed this morning or any morning for the rest of my life! Whatdahell has making your bed got to do with finding a new direction to your life? I'm free associating, okay? I'm in the moment, and all conventions are my enemy. I'm frustrated. No, I'm plenty pissed off. I've lived a half century, developed some pretty good marketable skills, went to church a lot, always drove below the speed limit, practiced the Golden Rule, and believed all those quotations my father hung up on my bedroom wall that said hard work brings you a happy ending. So wheredahell is my payoff? Instead I'm just another displaced person in a world turned upside down by a lot of money-grabbing, juicehead sideshow freaky baby boomers who've elevated irresponsibility and the pursuit of orgasms to a religion. I'm a child of the forties. I was born in the age of heroes. I'm a charter member of the Tom Mix Ralston Cereal Straight Shooters Club. We helped old ladies across the street; we didn't mug them. Sure we worshipped man-gods with funny names like DiMaggio, Ruth, Robinson, and the Lone Ranger, but they never let us down; they taught us about teamwork, dedication, and holding on to your integrity in tough times. And we didn't abuse the English language by saying people who boozed or took drugs had a "chemical dependency." No, we just called them what they were, stupid. And we were just naïve enough to think that nobody owed us a living just because we were poor or black or didn't speak English. Everybody worked and finished school, because that was the only way we knew to become better than we were. If you slept around, had babies before you could afford them, and sponged off your parents, you were a bum, because that's what bums did. You picked up after yourself, threw your trash in the garbage pail, not in the street, and said "please" and "thank you" because that's what decent people did. There were rules and regulations. Right and wrong. A clear direction to follow if you wanted to be a productive human being. And no one had to "find himself" or "get his shit together," because we always had a bathroom mirror to "find ourselves" and a mother schooled in Prussian discipline who never let our shit go beyond the kitchen table.

If you need it all tied up in a simple package, here it is: care was the glue that held us all together. Respect was always the uniform of the day. I've read and reread Voltaire's *Candide* about the man who searched all over the world for the right answer on how to lead a valued life. And I know what he concluded after all his tortuous years of searching: "I must tend to my own garden." Fine. But what do you do, Mr. Candide, when your garden is filled with a bunch of creepy, crawly, airhead, thirty-something yuppies in tight pants with no pockets who play loud music in their cars, eat raw fish, and think personal responsibility is the name of a new rock group?

Yeah, I'm angry. I'm angry I have to sit in a treehouse 2,500 miles away from my home trying to regain something I never should have lost in the first place. I'm angry my world is over and I have to find a new way in "their" world. I'm angry because I've been making my bed for the last three weeks. There's no logical reason to ever make a bed. It serves no purpose of taste or utility. It's not even in the same ballpark as putting a lid on a pot of stew to lock in the flavor or putting on a toupee or pulling down the lid on the privy. It's form without substance. It's an unchallenged tradition, a folly probably started by one of those obnoxious Chaucer characters from medieval Canterbury—probably the barrel-bottom Miller's wife sublimating her sex drive while hubby roams the hamlets boffing every dame that isn't kneeling in church. Oh boy, I'm angry. By God, I'm a free man far from the cry of absurd convention. I live in a treehouse! Did Tarzan make his bed?! Hell no. I'm not making mine. I'm going for a walk to the twenty-mile marker, God. And I want my answer before I get back.

But first, a shower, shave, and some Cream of Wheat. And no more Mr. Nice Guy of the forest. I'm going to get to that big, juicy mango on the ground before that furry glutton, Donaghy. I do, and it tastes great. No guilt.

Then, then ... dammit! I can't stand it anymore. Compulsion and fifty years of Judeo-Christian conditioning overcome me—has my passionate declaration of simplicity and freedom all been a false cry from a man without the grit to live his dream of obedience to no convention but his own spontaneity?! Has life on this idyllic isle eroded the very steel foundations to my liberated *raison d'être* ... what in God's name has come over me— I'm making my bed!

12

Are Windsurfers Messengers from God?

Ten minutes later. . .

I'm still angry as I head up the coast road. Mert and Marge are alongside. John Muir is ten feet behind. Mert steps on my foot. His navigational equipment is failing. He's old, half-blind, and has a busted nose that can't smell anymore. I prefer to think he's talking to me. I can hear him saying, "Cool it, pal. You're too filled with yourself to receive any messages from The Big Guy. Mellow out."

Mert is right. We all stop as I take several deep breaths of Molokai serenity.

I've picked an idyllic stretch of the island for possible Divine intercession. Two miles of heart-stopping beauty weaving through cool green valleys, giant amphitheaters reaching through the clouds to the top of Kamakou and tiptoeing down to smooth, sandy beaches. Every unique blush of the tropics is represented: shimmering green volcanic coral, soft yellow of the plumeria, rich redness of the blooming hibiscus; the muted scarlet and browns of the fertile shoreline soils—a kaleidoscope of color, constantly changing shape and texture with every push and pull of the trade winds.

We stop in front of the Gospel Shoes of Jesus Christ Church and Fruitstand. I figure any church that gives away fruit has a clear notion of salvation and must surely have the favor of the Lord. We wait. We doze. Nothing. We push onward past inlets and ancient town sites with names like Kapukapuahakea, Pauwalu, Puniu'ohua Nui Gulch, and Honouli Wai Bay, where we can now see Cape Halawa, the easternmost tip of the island. Still no voices. No messages.

We sit on the steps of the historic wood-framed Waialua Congregational Church, founded 1822, "Continuing the Mission in the Sandwich Islands." We have an unobstructed view east and west of the road. Not another living thing stirring. Four unlikely pilgrims, alone, waiting.

Suddenly, a mile or so out in the rowdy Pailolo Channel dividing Molokai from Maui, appears a lone windsurfer, gripping a red, blue, and yellow sail. Strange. I didn't see him on our trip up the coast. I couldn't have missed him. My eyes rarely left the seaward horizon. Where did he come from? And why, with such an ideal, powerful wind, is there only one of his kind?

Mert, Marge, Muir, and I watch his winged acrobatic ballet. I'm fascinated. Twenty, twenty-five knots of wind ripping, pulling, pounding; churning whitecaps washing his body, holding enough power in each spray to fling him effortlessly into the jagged coral formations all around him. There he goes south, southwest on a following wind. A renegade burst of turbulence from the lee of Cape Halawa catches him in a midair flip and instantly reverses his direction. And that's the way it goes time and time again—unpredictable bursts of air, first this way, then that way. And all the while the lone wind rider offers no resistance to the overpowering primal forces swirling around him. He simply holds his sail firmly and willingly allows things greater than himself to guide him to new directions. Into the sun. Toward the beach. Downwind, upwind, crosswind, and spurts of becalment. He accepts them all and seems to relish the chaos. It's quite difficult to see a smile on a face at this distance, but joy is easily recognizable at twice this length. It's definitely there.

Soon the wind decides to end its roaring bursts of surprises and settles on one point of origin. Or does it? Maybe the wind sailor just finds a comfortable tack, I'm not sure. He moves with a gentle flutter out past the reef into the open sea headed for I don't know where. It has been rumored that a few world-class veterans have successfully windsurfed this notoriously treacherous gulf between the islands. But under these storm-like conditions? I doubt it. Mert, Marge, Muir, and I are standing now on the ancient moss rock wall surrounding the church, watching our lone surfer. Finally, at one with a commanding wind, he flies off into the early morning channel mist. Soon the horizon swallows his sail.

Strange.

I return to the treehouse, discouraged I have not heard what Thoreau, Emerson, and London promised I would hear . . . the Divine whisper.

Or did I? Maybe the Voice sometimes takes flight on the amorphous breath of the wind, forming a simple message with the help of a red, blue, and yellow sail in the hands of a true believer. I wonder.

13

What's So Funny About Getting 90,000 Volts Shot Through Your Brain? Everything, If You Look Hard Enough!

I'm dying. The pain is unbearable.

A giant black tumor with large spider-like tentacles is lodged in the upper left frontal lobe of my brain and is systematically sucking my life force from me.

A few weeks ago I slipped on a rock exploring a waterfall in Maui and the tumor was born. Until now I've been able to battle the pain with "The Best of Harry James," The Andrews Sisters, and my Burns and Allen tapes. No more. I'm dying.

And don't give me that "How do you know it's a tumor? Maybe you've just got a migraine" bit.

When you're fifty, there are no more headaches. Just tumors. And I've got one.

So I fly to Honolulu to see Doctor Dan. He takes my family history, shines his coal miner's headlight into my eyes, and then tells me to drop my drawers and bend over the table. While I fail to understand the brain-tush connection, like all moderns I bow to the murky magic of science and comply.

He probes and immediately proclaims, "I'm seventy-five percent certain you don't have a brain tumor."

"Gee, Doc. I didn't think you went that far up."

He's a firm believer in the power of humor to heal. He laughs.

"What about the other twenty-five percent?" I ask.

He bites his lip, pauses, and replies, "We'll schedule you for a CAT scan next week."

I take more tests. Leave blood, urine, and a bag of popcorn for the nurses—assured they would know the difference—and head back to Molokai with a twenty-five percent certainty I am dying from a brain tumor.

Next week has arrived. Time to shoot 90,000 volts of electricity through my throbbing brain to confirm the obvious—death will end my search for meaning. I want my ashes scattered beneath the treehouse in Molokai. Erase that! Muir's too smart. He'd know and get the last laugh relieving himself all over my remains. I'll go to Arlington. Whatdaheck, it's time I used some of my GI benefits.

I approach the plump, bronze Hawaiian lady at the Diagnostic Imaging reception desk and suddenly become the class clown. Nerves, I guess.

"Howdy. I've been a good boy. Got up every four hours of the night to take my 50 mgs of prednisone[1] pills. No breakfast. Stomach's empty as ordered, and here I am taking my pre-scan capsule of Benadryl. My forms are all filled out, and look at that clock. Am I a good little boy? Ten sharp. Precisely on time."

She's a sunshine warrior. She hands me a lollipop.

"You are indeed a good little boy. Only one problem. You're twenty-four hours early. Your appointment is for tomorrow at ten."

I check the appointment card. Smiling, bronze Hawaiian lady is right.

The CT technician comes out and announces I'm in luck. They have a cancellation. The scheduled patient died during the night. I can take his slot. Swell! And if his clothes fit, I might as well take them, too. Whatdahell, when lady luck comes calling, you might as well grab as much as you can.

Now a CAT scan, like most dehumanizing medical tests, is a very scary thing. And Cindy, the milk-white technician in the Prince Valiant hairdo and pea green earth shoes, is very comfortable in this Dr. Frankenstein school of medicine. She frowns. She mumbles. She avoids direct eye contact, and she sighs on every exhale.

Three weeks in a treehouse has not changed my one absolute piece of knowledge learned in fifty years of hard city living—there is absurdity in every human experience. Birth, marriage, death, IRS audits, and everything

---

1   Pre-medication to reduce the possibility of a violent reaction to the iodine dye shot through your brain to give a sharper contrasting X-ray.

undertaken by serious, sanctimonious, uptight people. I've always figured my mental health depended upon my finding it before the black hats revoke my parade permit.

Cindy Milk White stops at the entrance to the scan lab. She sighs and ceremoniously asks, "Is there anything you want to know?"

I return the sigh and answer, "Yes. Metaphysically speaking, do you think there were any good Nazis?"

Her care plan obviously includes being a lousy listener. She didn't hear a word I said.

She leads me into a milk-white room where the equally milk-white Computer Tomography Scanner is the lone occupant, along with a small Ansel Adams photograph of Sunset on the Prairie. I study it. "Interesting environmental design. What's on the flip side, 'Death on the Trail'?" She's still not listening. She's pointing to the ominous giant white doughnut that will surely confirm my imminent demise. She speaks like a gunnery sergeant explaining the M-16 rifle to Neanderthals. "The Scanner is essentially a big X-ray machine, capable of focusing on a specific part of the anatomy, herewith your brain. It snaps a picture and feeds it to a computer that analyzes the data and constructs images on a TV monitor. You simply lay down on a slab; we strap you in and slide you into the center of the machine. Please strip down to your shorts."

"I can't until you leave the room herewith. I'm Catholic."

The character lines around her mouth start to crack. Not a smile, but close.

I lie down on the slab. Still no absurdity in sight, just a sea of whiteness and the early signs of an erection. It must have come from the slow way Cindy Milk White is strapping me down. My God, I'm a closet S&M freak!

She flips a switch and the two-million-dollar marvel roars into operation.

I make small talk while 90,000 volts prepare to shoot through my brain searching for the black spider tumor.

"So, tell me about this machine."

"Not much to tell. Been around fourteen or fifteen years. Considered a major breakthrough in science. Made by General Electric."

I muse, "Miracle technology, made in America. That's strange. Must use Fuji film."

Now comes the smile, "Right. How'd ya guess?"

Now comes the absurdity inherent in every single human act. She lays my head down on this superstar of science and routinely asks, "Is everything comfortable?"

The answer is "NO!"

The brilliantly crafted plastic sling that cradles your head is obviously on loan from the Tower of London. It pinches, intrudes, and hurts like hell.

Cindy Milk White searches for relief and comes up with three used kitchen sponges. No relief, just the smell of Ivory Liquid soap.

I'm laughing out loud. Cindy wants to know why.

"A two-million-dollar wunderkind of science able to leap into your brain at the speed of light and release secrets known only to Divine Intelligence, has a headrest designed by Pee Wee Herman. That's why."

Now that's absurd.

It's over. I'm still laughing. So I'm gonna die. So what. God was good. He sent a sign. Charlie Chaplin was right when he said, "In the end, it's all a joke."

Young Dr. Soon, the serious radiologist in the brown, color-coordinated polyester outfit, invites me to look at the inside of my brain. I do. I heartily recommend it for all of my kind. The Grand Canyon is nice. So are the pyramids and the 1969 Mets. All miracles. But strictly second team. Not until you look at the ten billion cells, incredibly protected in three pounds of spongy nervous tissue that power the fragile phenomenon of your own breath, can you begin to appreciate the only real major league miracle there is—life. Why? I think because when you look at the brain you suddenly realize what you can't see. You can't see fear, hate, the need to succeed, and ultimate meanings of things. It just doesn't show up on the X-ray. Because it doesn't exist in the hardware. Like the magnificent computer it is, all that software stuff has to be programmed in. And that's entirely up to the operator. That's what I'm seeing. It's a rare moment of light.

I'd rate it right up there with witnessing birth and watching the slow death of a loved one to learn everything you need to know to succeed at the next moment of life. Suddenly every other issue in the universe is trivial. Now that's real education.

I look a long time. So does Dr. Soon before he speaks.

"Looks good. No bleeding. No tumor."

He takes a long pause, moves closer to the X-ray for a final probe, and finally announces, "Yup. No doubt, there's nothing there."

I retort, "Thanks, Doc. You've just confirmed what Sister Mary Petrie knew all along."

He's puzzled. "Who's she?"

"My first grade teacher."

He notices a new medical problem.

"From the way you are holding your head, you seem to have a severe neck pain. May I be of assistance?"

"Sure, Doc. Buy a couple of new sponges, willya!"

He blushes. I start to leave. A sudden flash of the obvious hits. I turn and ask, "Say, Doc, got any idea what's causing these headaches?"

He takes a deep breath, removes his brown-rimmed glasses with the yellow tint, and very seriously offers, "Modern living, probably."

Sitting at the bus stop across from Honolulu's oldest church, Kawaihao, I wait for my ride to the airport. The 150-year-old belfry is alive with electronic music:

'Ekolu mea ina ka homua
'Oka mana 'o'i'o, ka alana
'A me ke alona, ke 'aloha ka'i.

(Three important things in the world. . .
Faith, hope, and Aloha. Of all three,
Aloha is the best.)

For whom the bells toll? Why, they toll for thee.

14

Paradise Interruptus

A major setback with my adventure with tranquility. I've got to return to Los Angeles to climb a very silly mountain.

The second largest HMO (Health Maintenance Organization—folks who run medical plans) in the West has contracted me to give a major workshop for their over-stressed top executives and are not now buying my cancellation due to a mid-life crisis as a valid reason not to sue me into submission. I suppose we'll never be truly free as long as one contract attorney is alive.

The uptight personnel director on the phone is really the universal voice of business and represents the single most uncomplicated reason Corporate America will never heal itself.

"Bob, please don't have us do any of that touchy-feely stuff. We're very conservative (that's execu-speak for in-human). And please don't split us up into small problem-solving groups. And, eh—please don't ask provocative questions about our employer-employee relations, and only limited interaction stuff."

I interrupt. "How about shaking hands?"

She pauses. "Eh, I'll have to check with my boss."

The title of the seminar: Increasing Productivity Through Open Communications.

I can hardly wait to joust with this thriving absurdity of our times.

Day One Back in Hell

(**Author's Note**: As incredulous as the following diary of a single day's events may seem, I raise my hand to the heavens and swear they happened precisely as I recorded them.)

I'm apprehensive. How will I react to the tolerated insanity of city captivity again? Will I revert to my old ways? Will the aches and pains return? Or have I crossed the bar to a sunnier place?

My new Molokai habit of a complete uninterrupted night's sleep carries over. So far so good.

6:15 a.m.

The assault begins. Small arms fire in the form of a shrill off-key duet of Benito Juarez's favorite revolutionary ditty, "La Paloma," sung by Ernesto and Son, the loudest gardeners in Southern California. Next comes the heavy artillery, the mechanized rumble from hell, the scourge of early morning serenity all across America, Armageddon's weapon of choice in the final destruction of our society—the leaf blower!

Breakfast, light exercise, lots of coughing. A second-stage smog alert coupled with stifling 104 degree moist heat is making breathing a priority concern.

8:45 a.m.

Business meetings. Coming down in the elevator. Doors open at the ninth floor and a plumber carrying the tools of his trade squeezes in. The group noticeably pulls back from him. A baby-faced heavyweight dripping with honest sweat, he looks at all the Italian-cut suits and imitation Gucci handbags and apologizes, "Sorry."

For what? Earning $45 an hour keeping the arteries of modern existence unclogged and freely flushing? What's the matter with you, son? Stand tall! What you do is infinitely more ennobling to the preservation of the tribe than this dehydrated blend of joyless paper pushers. You're not a searcher, a doubter, a sad-eyed compromiser selling out for privileged parking, gold-plated watches, and vapid elegance. And stop hanging your head! For God's sake, man. You're the last hero we've got performing the only clearly meaningful work left to us—manual labor. You have none of the sickening smallness of this smirking, trendy lot. You know what you're doing is necessary. You see the meaning every time you plug a leak, loosen a valve, or create a fitting. You walk in a world these people only dream of—instant gratification. You're the natural evolution of our rightful mission, simplify and complete the "now." You're a leader, a chieftain, a meat eater. Raise your head, show your plumber's pride, man!

He doesn't. He reaches his floor, meekly contorts his body to avoid making contact with his disdainers, and again apologizes . . . "Sorry."

The door closes. The gal in front of me with a Mohawk coiffure, cracking gum and wearing that sullen stare of a lost generation, waves her arms in front of her as if she's dispelling an ill wind. She intones, "There ought to be a separate elevator for people like *that*. For sure."

We continue our downward flight in silence. The men pretending not to be looking for cleavage, nipple protrusion, and panty lines. The women pretending not to notice the boys pretending.

Ground floor. My enraged value system needs requieting. Coldcocking Ms. Mohawk is beyond my new Molokai mellow. I opt for a less frontal assault. I goose her with my attaché case. Not the mousy wimpish one that school boys disguise as an accidental pat. No sir. This is the wind-up-and-jam-it-in-good kind like Grandpa did to you every time you made the mistake of going up the stairs in front of him.

Wow! Yelping like a timber wolf in heat, Arrogant Lady jumps out of her left spiked heel. Everyone turns to me for an explanation. I dutifully contort my body and meekly offer, "Sorry, they ought to have a separate elevator for guys like me."

What's happening? Why am I suddenly becoming a fight-back consumer? I've got to press the hold button until I return to my treehouse.

There's more city madness ahead.

1:15 p.m.

Driving back to my modest four-room country cottage by the park. The test to stay detached from the city frenzy is straining. I stop at a red light at the corner of my street. Ahead of me a tough-looking Latino female leans out the passenger side of her multi-bruised black and pink '65 Chevy and screams a litany of obscenities at the flawlessly smooth fuschia '79 Buick alongside me.

The driver, another tree-trunk-thick, red-hot mama leans out and returns the ornery fusillade. I cope as I always do in the circus dementia that is big city traffic. I punch up Benny Goodman "Stompin' At The Savoy." Benny fails me. The dueling muchachas are through shouting. They're shooting at one another! Wait a minute. This is not Tombstone Territory. This is hardworking, affluent middle-class, tree-lined Studio City, in Southern California.

Luckily they shoot about as well as they look. No direct hits. I pull off onto my street and never look back. Unfortunately, the other noncombatant motorists do the same. Are we all co-conspirators in the systematic collapse of the greatest social experiment in the history of life? Has the price of involvement become too great a tab to pay?

I strike a blow for enlightened citizenry. I call the police. They put me on hold. One minute and seven seconds later I hang up. The silent majority just registered another member.

3:40 p.m.

A knock at the door. It has an urgent quality. I check the peephole. A short fat man with a Buffalo Bill mustache and a mismatched green tie for his baggy black suit is twitching on my front step. Try as I do, I can't think of any ax-murderer or a single serial killer with a handlebar mustache and the body of Dr. Ruth, so I take a chance and open the door, cautiously.

He thrusts a large book in my face and speaks with a thick Mid-Eastern accent.

"Scented encyclopedias. Go ahead. Turn to any country and sniff."

"I'm really not in the mood to smell Yugoslavia, pal."

He gives me the obligatory snake oil smile, closes his perfumed book of knowledge, and beckons to his locomotive-size companion nearby that it's time to move the con elsewhere. They do. I watch. Something doesn't feel right. Genuine suspicion, or am I still in shock from my up-close brush with a standstill drive-by shooting? I'm not sure, but something.

3:55 p.m.

Corporate America calls. It's the personnel director of my HMO client. She's deathly afraid my billing as "America's Number One Fun Motivator" is real, and that I'm going to attempt to make her 147 beaten sheep actually enjoy communicating with one another.

"Bob, I just want to make certain you won't ask any of our executives to, you know, talk to one another . . . like in some kind of exercise or game. You know what I mean?"

"Yes, of course. You mean you want me to talk about the critical value of open communications, but not to demonstrate it."

Her squeaky voice becomes a whisper.

"Bob, may I confide in you?"

For the fee she's paying me, I assure her she may.

"Both our chairman of the board and our president are not 'people' type leaders, you know what I mean?"

I know precisely what she means. She means they're snobs, elitists, old world bankers with little minds and boxcar egos and a sickening comfortableness with the power to intimidate. She means they would rather rule than lead, dictate than coach, confound rather than simplify. Be ivory-towered and cut off from the one and only hope of economic solvency this nation has in these transition times—the creativity and emotional buy-in of its workers on the line.

This is not an atypical conversation. I have spoken to and consulted with over 1,500 business enterprises in this country (some very big and some very small), and the routine seldom varies from this.

And herein lies the greatest single moronic irony in the whole New Age economy—in a *Star Wars* era glorifying and profiteering from instant communications, we have at the helm of our corporate ships of state a group of captains who, by and large, do not, cannot, and will not reach out and talk, simply talk, to their work team.

Why?

Because they've never been taught that board chairmen and CEOs are people, too. They've never been taught they are the single most powerful determinant of what direction this country will follow, because their workers take their attitudinal cues from "the tower." If the boss is tight-lipped and removed, why should I care about increasing productivity?

Truly, every shred of my experience with management has repeatedly validated this simple morsel. Productivity starts with care. And care starts with talking straight to one another, simply and openly.

Poor, overly burdened Madam Personnel Director caps the folly with, "But they're both medical doctors, so I guess that explains it all."

I assure her I will abide by her rules on nonengagement and remain as unemotional in my "lecture" as a Zen Buddhist in a coma.

I lie.

15

Long Day's Journey Into Night Gets Longer

5:10 p.m.

When I started this book, I pledged to share all my thoughts with you on this mid-life venture. I report the following events in that original spirit of commitment.

An indelicate matter of personal hygiene. A severe case of fungi intertrigo, jock itch. It suddenly flares as I'm outlining tomorrow's seminar. With head, heart, and eyes buried in my seminar notes, I reach for the soothing relief of a 3.5-ounce can of anti-fungal spray. I generously apply it to the affected area.

Wow!

How can anything so good for you hurt so badly? My loins are swelling geometrically. The rash is spreading like a brush fire in August.

What's going on here?

What's going on is I missed the relief can and instead grabbed an economy-size can of Raid Ant and Roach

Killer and sprayed enough dicholoro-ethenyl on my man-hood to defoliate the Alaskan tundra. Wow! Owww!

Dash outside in the yard and apply the garden hose to my fire down below. Aww, momentary relief. Wait a minute. I'm not alone in this burlesque.

My next-door neighbors, two somber septuagenarian widows, have dropped their afternoon patio iced tea and are staring in confused horror.

Telling the truth will not make me free. I choose stupidity over veracity.

"Only thing that seems to cool me down on days like this."

They give the "grandma smile." You know the one. You got it when you introduced her to your first bimbo and followed it with, "We're just friends, honest."

The copy line on the Raid can reads, "Kills on contact—keeps on killing." Truth in advertising. My upper thigh muscles are corroding. Suddenly I'm bowlegged. Swell, maybe I'll put on a Stetson tomorrow, carry a lariat, and do rope tricks at the seminar. Surely that would open communications.

6:20 p.m.

My genuine, authentic 1934 ceiling fan is outmatched by 107 stifling degrees of heat. I seek relief at a refrigerated movie show.

Pack an ice bag for my super-heated welted loins, and bowleg my way to see Robin Williams in *Dead Poets' Society*. Forty-five minutes early. Buy a ticket. Third in line, should get a good seat. My ice is melting. Refill at the concession stand. Back in line.

Young lovers behind me and senior citizens ahead of me give me a wide berth. A grown man in an aloha shirt and shower shoes holding a tub of ice against his genitalia sounds their "freak alarm." Can't blame them.

The line soon grows to 200 plus. As we start to move into the theater, two young super-trendy females in electra-glow outfits brazenly push their way to the head of the line and move ahead of me. I politely point out their injustice. Without missing a crack of her gum, one of them, the one in the black leather mini-skirt, green earrings, and "Shit Happens" T-shirt, characterizes, perhaps, a whole generation with, "We're children of the eighties. We don't care. We're material girls." They laugh.

The fire in my loins has transferred to my brain. I'm blowing my Molokai mellow. I can't maintain the role of detached observer any longer. I turn around and plead my case to my fellow victims. But they don't care, either. The "I-don't-give-a-damners" are becoming the new majority.

7:41 p.m.

The manager of the theater asks me to leave. I do . . . with a smile.

Why?

Because I got inspired by Robin Williams' character constantly telling his in-movie students to "carpe diem!" (seize the day). Because a half hour into the movie, when he jumps up on his teacher's desk and admonishes a beat generation to ". . .seize their moments and make them count to ennoble and inspire good things," I moved to the row behind the two "material girls" and dumped two giant-size cherry Slurpies all over their unconcerned material heads, shoulders, cleavage, laps, and feet. One shouted Robin Williams down with, "You asshole. What-dahell did you do that for, dorkface?"

I replied with surprising calm, "Hey, man, shit happens."

Carpe diem!

8:20 p.m.

Back to my cottage.

Police are questioning one of my septuagenarian neighbors. She's been robbed. I ask what happened.

"Some guy broke through my screen doors, stole my TV while I was sitting in the kitchen."

"Did you get a look at him, ma'am?" asks one of the cops.

"Kinda short, fat guy with a big mustache. He smelled funny."

The con now has a name.

A few moments of quiet reflection. Are the events of this day aberrations or the new order of things? Has kindness and consideration given way to a wave of material girls and cool dudes on a perpetual feeding frenzy of mindless pleasure? Have the dehumanizing shrills and zombie values of a drug-riddled generation overpowered the Golden Rule? Where does MTV end and real life begin? Or are they now one and the same?

I'm not even sure I should be concerned about finding an answer.

Click on the TV to catch the day's baseball results. Mercifully, I will end my first day back in civilization on a lighter note.

The gushing good fairy weatherman is shaking his head. "Tomorrow will be a scorcher, a record-breaking 108 degrees. Continued first-stage smog alert. People with respiratory ailments are advised to. . . ." Click off. To sleep, perchance to dream of a more tranquil life in a treehouse in a far off special place.

1:30 a.m.

Can't sleep. The pains in my head have returned.

16

Maybe All That Corporate America Needs Is a Good Recess Period

Today I face the corporation that wants to open communications . . . but not too much, lest the serfs start believing they're working in a democracy.

So why do they invite the fox inside the henhouse?

Because *absurdum est omnes vitae.*[1]

I arrive an hour early and seek relief from the hottest July 20th in Southern California history. I head for the one shade tree in the sprawling, spotlessly clean parking lot winding around a clump of futuristic structures—monorails, geodesic domes, and towering glass monoliths. Could very easily be an extension of Disney's Tomorrowland just a few miles down the road.

No Mickey and Minnie, but there is a Goofy, and here he comes. He's wearing a security guard's outfit, carrying

---

1   "Absurdity is all there is to life," or something like that.

forty pounds of electronic gadgetry on his shiny black patent leather belt. And he's Dick Tracy serious about reporting my every move over his shiny blue walkie-talkie.

He approaches my car with darting Marine Corps reconnaissance precision. There's no telling what damage a guy with bifocals in a three-piece, double-breasted Price Club special sitting in an '85 Nissan packed with helium-filled balloons inscribed "Lighten Up and Win" will do.

"Good morning, officer. I'm here to give a seminar for your corporate executives. I'm a little early. Thought I'd catch up on my notes."

He's suspicious. Looks at the balloons and then does a quick junior G-man visual check of the front seat for concealed assault weapons.

"I'm clean. The only weapon I've got on me today is the truth."

I smile. He's confused. I show him my letter from the president, the one with all the obligatory words like "team-building," "cooperation," and "quality care."

Confusion turns to disbelief.

He looks at the balloons.

"You mean yur gonna actually try to make our managers laugh!? Boy, good luck."

He laughs without changing expression or moving any muscle group in his body.

"Thanks. It's always nice to have the support of the troops on the front line."

I give him a balloon. He lights up like a kid in a candy store, drops his walkie-talkie, bends down to pick it up, loses the balloon, and bangs his head on my side view mirror. See, I knew it was Goofy all along.

Back to my notes. Another car pulls alongside to share the only shade available. Something strange going on. The driver, a full-figured woman with short hair in a red smock, dips down out of sight. In a few moments she reemerges with long hair and a black dress with big yellow flowers.

I'm witnessing a phenomenon of our transitional times—the hardship, strength, and magic of life on the Mommy Track. A role I'm sure no man can fully appreciate or long endure himself without lots of Divine assistance.

This supremely organized lady has shed her comfy mommy-in-the-morning costume for the stiff armor of executive female breadwinner in less than six minutes, and in a bucket seat, no less. Bravissima!

I'm about to congratulate her when I recognize that unmistakable look all heroes have when they battle excruciating pain with a feeble smile. It's a look that says, "I know I'm going to die, but I just won't let the world know about it." We've all worn it. It happened a hundred humiliating times at the beach when Mom would wrap a towel around us and unknowingly stunt our budding self-esteem by pulling off our wet bathing suit and shaking out a dry pair of underwear for all to see before slipping it underneath and onto our traumatized little bodies. As hard as she tried, she always batted less than .500 when it came to keeping our private parts hidden from public scrutiny. That's the look I'm seeing now. By Jehosephats, this lady is changing her underwear!

Out of respect for childhood memories, I turn 180 degrees due west and think clean thoughts.

Ten minutes to eight. Time to joust with corporate pretension. A sour-faced hostess leads me down to their catacombs and through a quarter mile of the whitest white subterranean level of any office building I have ever seen. I chat. She ignores me and points across the white corridor to a white door. "This is executive meeting room B1A." I expect to be handed a blindfold, offered a cigarette, and asked if I have any last requests. She turns abruptly and leaves. It always tickles me that we label this robotic behavior "professional."

I'm on my own.

Inside. A few of the early-bird senior managers are pecking at the sweet rolls and coffee. They're separated in silent cliques. Their body language is unanimous in declaring, "We're in for a full day of root canal work."

Here they are, the typical top-rung corporate executives, senior VPs, engineers, MBAs, doctors, nurses, administrators, department heads—the single most critical leadership factor in determining the economic survival of this nation—starchy, grim-faced, guarded dissidents wearing their obvious angst on their French cuffs like Apache funeral flags.

Don't let it fool you. Their basic need is the same as any other blue-collar working man or woman in this country—they want to enjoy their life at work and have their contribution openly applauded. And, typically, some medieval lord of the realm on the top floor is blocking all that.

There is no secret to how to motivate the New Breed Worker in the New Age Reality to produce more with less.

It comes down to a self-evident truth—show your team you really care! Be a human being. Let your people play, laugh, celebrate, suggest, and feel ownership for the final product or service. People today are in a desperate rage to know that the forty percent of their lives they spend at work counts for something. Let it, dammit!

It's the only management theory that works. In every single productivity problem I've investigated in twenty years of consulting, I've always found the root cause to be a boss who simply didn't know how to smile, tell the truth, praise, listen, share power, and say "thank you." We make instant millionaires of faddish "How To..." business gurus and their one-minute theory XYZ, Attila the Hun, MBO (Managing By Objective), work smart, managing chaos tactics. But ask any lover of life and long-term producer, and he'll tell you they're all afterthoughts dancing on the abyss, refurbished snake oil remedies, colorful tourniquets that may slow the bleeding but do nothing to heal the wound.

In 1980 the *New England Journal of Medicine* reported the astounding results of a long-term study of people at work: "Joy and satisfaction does more for a person's overall health and well-being than all the exercise and all the nutrition combined."

If managers don't know how to make people feel good about their jobs, every other style, strategem, and perk is as useless as a martini at a Baptist convention. We've got to lighten the grip and get back to basic running, blocking, and tackling. The proximate reason for all work is survival, but the ultimate motivator, the heart and soul of all productivity, is and always will be to feel good about yourself.

"Non-people-type" managers are the root causes of America's productivity problems, not the Japanese, not sudden global competition, not dwindling markets. The American worker has a Promethean history of extraordinary creativity, endurance, adaptability, and muscle under death-defying circumstances including two World Wars that threatened the very life of the planet. They won then, and they can surely handle the present woes, but only if their basic fuel—caring leadership—is right there on the line smiling, explaining, sharing, leveling, and "high five-ing" the winners.

All this is whirling through my brain as a frail, well-tailored lady in a charcoal gray business suit and wearing a neck brace meekly tugs at my sleeve. She whispers an apology. "The chairman of the board and the president won't be here today. They, eh, scheduled other meetings." We both know she's running interference for two scaredy-cats. "Hi, I'm Clytemnestra, the personnel director. We talked on the phone."

The ashen-complected, nervous lady before me is about as far south of her alluring, strong-willed Greek mythological namesake as you can get. She's flat, worried stiff, and Irish. She holds a lace handkerchief to her thin lips the way one of those fading ladies in a Tennessee Williams play does.

She softly explains she's lost her voice and developed a severe neck pain, which the doctor thinks might be caused by stress. She turns and introduces me to the lady who will present me to the audience. "This is Clarissa, our vice president of marketing. She's a fun person."

She's wearing a stylish black dress with big yellow flowers and, presumably, wearing clean underwear. Small world.

The room soon swells to capacity. About 200.

Clytemnestra gives me a final-minute warning before tiptoeing to the last seat in the back row. "Remember, we're very conservative. No music, getting up, moving around, you know, the touchy-feely stuff. I know you've been in this kind of situation before and know precisely how to handle it."

I pat her clammy right hand and assure her I do, indeed, know what to do.

I stick my "Hooked On Swing" cassette in the audio player, turn it up full, and watch Glenn Miller work his magic. Immediately people are smiling, talking, acting human. Clytemnestra is choking on her handkerchief.

Next I cut the petrified personnel director's life expectancy in half.

"The overriding theme of our seminar this morning can best be expressed by an ancient Greek philosopher who said (I reveal a large quotation of the flip chart and read it aloud), "If things aren't funny, then they are what they are . . . and life becomes one long dental appointment." I've signed it, Clytemnestra O'Hara. The group howls in delight. Miss O doesn't know if the pains in her chest are cardiac arrest or just the sudden withdrawal of starch.

From here it's all downwind sailing. We touch, we talk openly, we pat one another on the back, we form small "Fun-storming" groups, get to know precisely who everybody in the room is and what they need for better cooperation. Time now to take off our Pierre Cardin jackets, loosen our rep ties, kick off our three-quarter heel pumps, and play the game of open communications. We do, for four hours. We act out the part of the three top managers at NASA involved in the critical decision to ignore the now infamous O-ring deficiency and launch the *Challenger* spacecraft on its 1986 ill-fated, short flight to tragic immortality. We learn the managers at NASA were afraid to communicate with their bosses. We learn some bosses only like to hear good news. We learn that unless everybody in a business is free to talk and to listen to everybody else, then trust and loyalty is a fable.

Department heads who never talked to one another are now talking. Conflicting egos are now laughing with one another and working out compromises. We are learning the four magic words that set any leader on the path to possibilities—"I need your help."

We end in a giant circle, arms locked around one another's waists shouting, "We are a winning team!"

Everybody is touching and feeling.

Clytemnestra is gleefully waving her neck brace high over her head with one hand and hugging a fellow worker with the other.

All kids are open communicators. You just have to let 'em come out and play.

17

Gecko-Mania Means Something Different in a Treehouse

Back in the treehouse. A-h-h-h-h . . . life has possibilities again.

A few words about geckos. They are the tiniest folk heroes in Hawaii. They're everywhere. On T-shirts, key chains, bathing suits, muumuus, underwear, and surfboards. They're sung about on the radio. Their likeness is blown up, stuffed, and placed on coffee tables next to those big, expensive picture books nobody reads. One high school has adopted it as its mascot. A local activist group is shouting all the time to elevate them right up there with the lei and the pineapple as the official symbol of Hawaii. Some even ascribe mystical powers to them, at least an omen of good fortune. All this adoration and affection for a soft-skinned, tropical lizard with a short, stout body, a large, ugly head, and suction pads on its feet.

Its sole purpose in life is to stalk, pounce upon, and eat any size insect it can get its gummy jaws on. If spiders, flies, cockroaches, and moths could talk, they'd tell you the gecko is the most effective hunter in the animal kingdom. Ounce for ounce they may also be the biggest eaters, too.

But what goes in must come out.

As I look around my modest retreat, I discover another stunning characteristic of these tiny mighty mites. They are the most prolific defecators in the forest primeval. Their mark is everywhere. And if their droppings are as energy-producing as their larger paleolithic predecessors, my living room could fuel a few dozen manned space flights to galaxies unknown.

I clean for three hours and still haven't made a dent. A herd of the little doo-doo monsters is looking in at me from my bedroom window. They're making an uncharacteristic sound. Not their trademark strong, high-pitched clicking noise; something else, light, shrill.

Wait a minute! The buggers are laughing at me! That's it, they're laughing.

I strike back by spraying the lot with a few king-size whiffs of my Brut underarm deodorant. Doesn't faze them one bit. Probably all I've done is enhance their love lives a few notches.

Nightfall.

Muggy August is no respecter of paradise. Its sweaty tentacles have wrapped around the trade winds, muffled its chimes, and changed the music of the night. All is still, except the sound that never fades—nature's most consistent herald—the roll, crest, and thunder of wave upon shore. The sleeping pill of the gods.

It's working on one jet-lagged mortal in a treehouse. But first a little good-night reading. Still open on the nightstand is Henry Thoreau's *Walden Pond*.

Would that I could harness the simple poetry he found to describe the life around him and his clear response to it:

> "I had this advantage at least, in my mode of life, over those who were obliged to look abroad for amusement, to society and the theater, that my life itself has become my amusement and never ceased to be novel . . . follow your genius closely enough and it will not fail to show you a fresh prospect every hour."

What sweeter lullaby could you ask for?

Still, I turn the page for more.

Good Lord! No, not possible! Not in the middle of these sainted thoughts. Yes, there it is. But how? To find the grit and muscle to actually turn a ten-weight bonded page in a Random House Modern Library edition, and to have the audacity to deposit waste matter on classic structure . . . and then to turn the page back again?!

The legend of the mighty gecko grows.

Sorry, Henry.

18

Beatin' Da Congas Fo' Da Lord

John Muir reads Jack London.

He sits on the outside sill of the screened porch, looking over my shoulder. But only when I'm reading Jack's *Tales of the South Seas*. It's getting so every time I turn the page, I check to see if Muir is finished. The darn cat's got me spooked.

But the gap between us is narrowing. About three yards.

Sunday morning.

Thin sheets of mist blowing in from Maui. All of Molokai is transformed into a giant rain forest strengthening the perfume of the gods, the most seductive fragrance in the tropics, my wake-up call as it is gently pushed through my treehouse every morning by the accommodating trades, the combined scents of delicate jasmine and enticing gardenia, and the smell that found its way into the writings of every great writer-adventurer who visited the islands, from Captain Cook to Mark Twain and James Michener . . . *white ginger!*

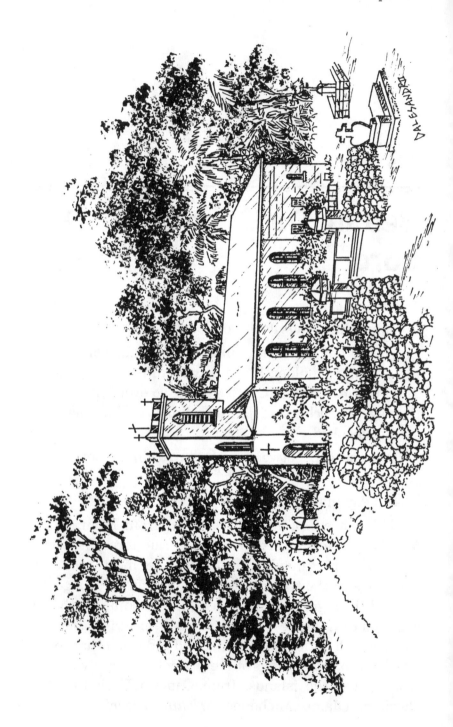

A-h-h-h-h-h.

Every Sunday I attend a different church service.

Why?

I'm not sure. I'm not looking for God. I never lost Him. Maybe when you're fifty you suddenly become truly ecumenical and want to cover all the bases. Or maybe when you live on an island with one church for every one hundred residents you just get nosy about the need for variety.

Many of the "churches" are little more than a cardboard sign hung in the window of a quonset hut home every Sunday morning. The names are intriguing— "Swinging Door to Jesus"; "Aloha Pathway"; "Christian Buddhists in Nature"; "The Ilima Family Hands to Heaven." But my favorite remains my neighbor to the east, "Gospel Shoes of Jesus Church and Fruitstand."

I hear them before I see them. They're singing and clapping their way through endless choruses of "Blood of the Lamb" to the improbable accompaniment of conga drums, ukuleles, and Brazilian maracas.

I walk up the muddy hill, past the rotting fishing dinghy, the empty fruit stand, and the windowless '52 Plymouth to the lean-to pavilion church. Inside the old red-and-white wooden structure newly reinforced by a couple of bare 2x4s overhead is a typical Molokai congregation seated on simple wooden benches. Eight adults, a dozen keikis (kids), a lot of bare feet, and, now, one haole.

The sleeping pit bull at the foot of the makeshift pulpit is a new wrinkle. Four of the faithful are playing ukuleles. One is nursing a baby at the same time.

Hard to tell what denomination fits the Gospel Shoers. They clap like Quakers, sing like Southern

Baptists, wear the historical pained look of Jews, and take up collections like Catholics—every fifteen minutes.

Oh, boy, do they sing! Eleven songs in a row, all four verses of each, including the "Battle Hymn of the Republic."

One hour and thirty-five minutes into the service, the preacher takes the pulpit. He's an ancient Hawaiian warrior. Chiseled in bronze, strong, young, ramrod straight, with shiny black pearls for eyes. His constant broad smile would melt the doubts of any infidel. Speaking in the local pidgin dialect, he has the gift to enthrall with simplicity:

> "We all in da same out-riggah canoe. Diff-rent paddles, maybe, but all goin' in da same die-rection. Nobody can get dere any soon-nah by pullin' harder. We have to work to-gettah, find a reeth-em and work to make dat reeth-em stronger. Da team dat wins doesn't win because dey got da most muscles. Da win-nahs learn how to flow wit everybody else in da boat."

From the bulge of the massive triceps straining the sleeve openings of his faded pink aloha shirt, this preacher speaks from experience.

We cheer for Jesus, take turns on the congas, sing all four verses of ten more hymns, all with high impact aerobic clapping. My mitts look like three-day-old lasagna.

Next, one hour's worth of testimony revealing the congregation is all one family, the Kahees, living in three clapboard shacks behind the "church." Pure-blooded Hawaiians, they came to Molokai twenty-five years ago when Honolulu started adopting big city evils. Papa taught them to respect the aina (land), to hunt and fish for their food, and to keep their ohana (family) strong.

Kiulani, the eldest sister, jumps up to testify. The pit bull wakes up and growls. She gives him the evil eye, and he meekly retreats behind the conga drum.

"When we were keeds, Papa would load us into da canoe and paddle past da breakers into da ocean to fish. We stayed out a long time. Da waves would come, beeg ones, ten, twelve feet and get set fo' da bury us good. Remember how scared we get? Den Papa would start preechin' da word to does beeg buggers, and we jest figgah we all goners. Papa sez, 'no wave gonna beat ya if you believe, if you committed to da Lord.' Den he tell da waves fo' to stop. And whatdaya know? Pretty soon da sea is as calm as da fuzz on da peach. We all stunned. Not Papa. He jest sit back, smile and sez, 'da stronger da commitment, da smaller da wave.' "

An old man in front of me remembers and cries the way strong men do, from the inside first until feeling overpowers muscle, and lets it all out.

A small boy alongside him, wearing a T-shirt declaring "Gecko Power," runs up to the pulpit to look for tissues. There aren't any left. The heavyset lady with the shoulder tattoos in the first row used them all when she testified she used to be a big drinker and carouser until Jesus entered her life. He put a stop to her evil ways about the same time all the bars on Molokai closed for good. The little boy comes back to the old man's side, puts his hand gently on his shoulder, and whispers in his ear at the decibel level of a Civil Defense siren test, "No mo' left. You gotta use your sleeve." He does.

The next half hour everybody sprinkles their testimony with the hope all 6,000 islanders can pray together to keep the mainland developers from bulldozing the sacred aina and bringing in lots of people who don't care. My turn to testify. They only request I start by quoting a passage from the Bible. I do.

"Prayer alone is like a rainbow without the colors.
But prayer coupled with action gives the Lord a
chance to help. Pray and then do."

I make a passionate plea for this congregation to take action and join with every other congregation on the island and hold a "Unity Day" to alert everybody that the saddest chapter in Hawaiian history is about to be written: the fall of Molokai, the last pure bastion of aloha. They look at me and smile. They grab their Bibles and shout, "God will provide."

Their childlike trust has been their strength and their downfall as a people. For the history of these gentle, loving believers has been one of naïve capitulation to the outsider and his purposeful deception in defining "progress." First the English, getting their trade routes and sucking the local economy dry. Then the fishing fleets, disregarding sensitive ecology and overloading their hulls with the bounty of local species. Next the missionaries, who saved souls in exchange for the most fertile land in the Pacific. Their ancestors became bankers and real estate brokers who are now selling the land off to foreign speculators at the most enormous profit margin anywhere on the face of the planet.

The good Lord will have to provide a spectacular rearranging of their national character to prevent this final tragedy in the name of progress.

We end three hours and twenty-five minutes after the start of service by holding hands and singing "Bringing in the Sheaves." Four choruses.

The preacher puts his arm around my shoulder and softly asks, "I didn't recognize your passage. What part of the Bible did it come from?"

"The inside front cover, Book of Louie."

He smiles benignly, as if he understands. He doesn't. It's my father's inscription to me on my high school graduation day.

Back down the road to my secular life in a tree.

Uh oh, there she is again, the Hippie Lady (that's what Kane, the no-neck bus driver calls her) and her barefooted three-year-old son with a Mohawk hairdo just like the gal in the elevator. They're picking fruit at the seaward vegetation line.

She is an Indian maiden, dark, thin, lithesome, with the taut body of a Yoga teacher. She doesn't have that pasty, vacuous look of phony rapture one usually associates with the born-again child of flowers, but those Viet Cong black pajamas with the fading peace symbol on the right breast and the long, unfettered silky auburn hair flapping wildly down her back have earned her the name, Hippie Lady, at least from those who only know her at a distance.

There is great love between mother and child. You can see it in the in-between moments as she calmly explains the properties of every fruit they pluck.

I've seen them several times, foraging in the outback, but my east coast aversion to anything resembling Haight-Ashbury has turned me away from greeting them.

This moment is no exception. I bow my head to avert her smile and go my way. But I'm wrong, dead wrong, about this lady, who is soon to become a major factor in my rebirth in the forest.

19

Pluvialis Dominica! I've Found the Missing Link!

He conclusively proved to me 500 years of Western thought was all wet.

We met as a result of our mutual love of classical music.

Every morning, just before sunrise, I place my ancient flaking Magnavox cassette player on the east side windowsill facing the rising sun and play "Morning" from the *Peer Gynt Suite*, Opus 46, by Grieg. It's music's most precise glorification of the miracle of a new day.

One morning, just after the London Symphony under the direction of Sir Thomas Beecham began the transition from flutes and oboes into full orchestration, *he* appeared. A complete stranger to our environs, he sidled up to the outside windowsill opposite my aging music box, raised his short silken neck to the sky as if in response to some greater call, and started rocking back and forth to the sweet crescendo. He became a living metronome, a totally committed aficionado, picking up intensity with every flexion of Sir Thomas' baton.

He has joined my sunrise ritual ever since.

He's a discriminating chap. He'll stay glued to the windowsill as long as I follow Grieg with some Debussy, Mendelssohn, Chopin, or Pachebel's Canon, but as soon as I switch to the more pedestrian tones of Harry James or Artie Shaw, he unceremoniously turns his back and retreats to a ten-foot-square rocky area on the slope to the side of the treehouse.

He never told me his name. I never asked. So, in keeping with my established habit, I go against type and give him one—Henry Wadsworth Longfellow. He looked nothing like the celebrated nineteenth-century poet at all. In fact, he looked and acted more like Basil Rathbone, the supreme urbane actor of the forties who played Sherlock Holmes— confident, jaunty, economical in movement, a cerebral master of deductive logic.

Henry is a bird. What kind, I don't know. He looks like a pigeon on stilts and struts around with the air of a five-time winner on "Jeopardy." He's sort of off-white, but not really. Maybe, dusky gray. He has brown-leaning-toward-khaki-tipped wings with a kind of magenta breast, sorta faded fire engine red feet, and Jean Harlow white freckles on a toasted whole wheat beak. In my limited brush with ornithology, I have never seen his like before and might never had cared jot nor tittle about his family history until that amazing Thursday around 10:45 in the morning when I began the greatest learning experience of my life.

It started at sunrise when I looked out on a gray day with low-flying dark clouds portending an unusual summer storm. It never came, but the moody grayness continued and I decided to forgo my usual musical wake-up call. It was a minor decision. I thought nothing of it.

Obviously, Henry didn't feel the same way. I had interrupted the ebb and flow of his newly acquired taste, and he was going to let me know about it.

In our previous communications, Henry and I had an understanding—when he pecked several times in a row that meant he wanted something, usually more water in his bowl, another helping of whole wheat bread, something, and I would comply. This morning he's at my screen door, pecking near the latch. I open the door and he doesn't hesitate. He flies right to the top of the Magnavox, now located on the west side of the room, and starts pecking on the large round volume control knob.

Wait a minute, this is something that happens on the "Ed Sullivan Show," not in the forest primeval. What is he saying . . . he wants me to play his classical favorites? No, come on. Can't be. I wait. He pecks. I wait some more. He keeps on pecking. Finally, with the disbelieving look of a man who has just seen the Ghost of Christmas Past dancing on his bedsheets, I cautiously slip in my "Philharmonic Classics, Part I." The soft pianissimo of wind instruments and harps herald the coming sunrise in Grieg's "Morning." The pecking stops, and man and bird in this funny little confounding moment seem to be questioning a fundamental tenet of Western philosophy—is *Homo sapiens* the only sentient creature in nature that thinks? My answer comes quickly, and, to symbolize that new affirmation, I walk over, pick up my leather-bound Book of the Month Club edition of Wil and Ariel Durant's *History of Western Thought*, and throw it in the trash basket.

Living by the Pacific, surrounded by the bounty and wisdom of nature, has convinced me modern philosophy is all wet.

Why?

Because it is based on a false assumption—that only humans think and all other matter is unknowing and inert. That animals react to base instinct and nothing more.

All of this hypothesized by guys from the city who had gout-ridden patrons paying their bills while they watched life from a marble tower in the high-rent district.

From before the time of the Greek philosopher Thales, who lived in the sixth century before Christ, until the time of the French philosopher Rene Descartes, 1,600 years after Christ, most Westerners of learning thought that nature was alive and, at least loosely speaking, conscious.

Now I know they were right.

While I am the only human being on my one-acre plot by the sea, I am surely not the only one around here deducing and inducing knowledge from pure reason alone. Hell, I'm living with an opportunistic cat who judges my actions, an entrepreneurial mongoose who has decided to abandon a few centuries of genetic determinate eating habits, a pair of hotshot mynahs flawlessly executing standard Marine Corps field maneuvers to maintain their food supply, two pensioned canines who appreciate sunsets, and now a strange, cocky bird who prances up to the heretofore master of the universe and demands to hear the world's finest music.

It suddenly becomes apparent to me that I may be the lowest form of life around here.

The old questions of what happened to heroes, truth, justice, the old-fashioned American way, and will my prostate last into my sixth decade give ground to a new passion—finding out who is this uncanny bird? Does he represent the missing link in the evolution of our species, or is he a showbiz veteran on the lam from a Ringling Brothers side show?

The search begins.

I hitch a ride into Kaunakakai to the one-room library at the edge of town in the back of a camouflaged war surplus truck hauling a half-ton of limu (seaweed) to the wharf. After fifteen minutes I smell like the Jersey shore in late August. I care not. I am hot on the trail of one of the great mysteries of the universe.

Andrew J. Berger's *Encyclopedia of Hawaiian Birds* doesn't help much. Henry comes closest to a common garden variety pigeon, but the freckles and the whole wheat beak don't match.

I call the Audubon Society in Honolulu, who refer me to the Nature Conservancy on Molokai, who refer me to the Maui Birdwatcher's Society.

Mrs. Betty Yomiguchi has a sweet trill of a voice like one of the melodious thrushes she watches.

"He sounds sorta' like a spotted dove, or maybe a red-footed booby . . . but I'm not sure. What about his behavior?"

"Well, Henry is a strict vegetarian partial to sesame spaghetti, frozen canneloni, low-fat granola, peanut butter and jelly on whole grain bread, and lime Jell-O. He has impeccable table manners. He'll only eat off a plate. I tried leaving food on the ground but he never touched it. One day I brought out a plate with several entrées, and he's been eating on earthenware ever since. He's a moderate drinker, no water, only cold herbal tea."

She interrupts me, "What about his social behavior?"

"There's no Mrs. Henry, if that's what you mean, and he's a *Terminator* when it comes to combat. Twice John Muir has tried to put him on his à la carte menu and twice Henry nearly did him in. He'd wait until John had crept to within a few feet, then turn on him suddenly, puff out his chest, raise his wings to full span—about eighteen inches—and make a wild samurai charge at his nose. John won't even look at him now. Donaghy, the mongoose, whose ancestors ate the Hawaiian goose into extinction, stepped into the ring with him this morning and got TKO'd before he could throw a punch. Henry did a helicopter take-off and then a barrel roll dive on Donaghy's tail. Let's see, what else . . . he likes to ride on Marge's back and she lets him. Oh yes, I'm convinced this is a highly evolved thinking species."

There is a long pause and finally Betty speaks. The trill is gone and an uncertain tremolo appears. "Thinking?" Another pause and then, "I think you better call Dr. Herb Philanta of the Bishop Museum. He's spent forty years working with Hawaii's bird life. If he doesn't know, then . . . you have an alien on your hands."

Dr. Philanta speaks in machine-gun bursts, lets you know exactly what he's thinking—often unrelated—and doesn't wait for responses.

"Sounds like you've got an alien on your hands . . . could be a dove or a booby or even a pigeon . . . no, no, the freckles and the beak don't match . . . hmmm, larger than a mynah, smaller than a nene . . . a loner, you say, fearless, attacks a mongoose, my God! . . . 8,600 species of birds in the world, just when you think you know them all, an alien comes along . . . got to watch the time, have to pick up my daughter-in-law at Safeway or is it 7-Eleven, I'm not sure . . . do you think his legs are long enough to fit his whole body underneath them." He takes a breath. I jump in.

"I suppose if he were a contortionist he could. I wouldn't put it past Henry." Doctor Herb hasn't heard a word I said.

". . .two bands on his legs, you say, hmmm . . . somebody's doing a control study . . . only one I know of . . . no, no this bird couldn't be . . . no, no. . . ."

"Couldn't be what, Doc, what?" I shout into the receiver.

". . .Pacific golden plover, *Pluvialis dominica* . . . incredible bird . . . leaves the Alaska tundra in late July or August, flies thousands of miles against unbelievable odds and winters in Hawaii . . . heads back in March . . . may be the most intelligent bird in the world. . . ."

"That's Henry, Doc, I'm sure that's Henry."

I'm sure the good bird doctor never heard my "goodbye and thank you so much" as I hung up and headed back to *Berger's Bird Encyclopedia* where the mystery got murky again. Henry really didn't match the colored lithograph of the Pacific golden plover, but there was a clue hidden in a microscopic footnote: "Frequently a maverick appears without many of the descriptive characteristics, but a plover nevertheless."

In my book, any bird who prefers continental Italian cuisine and knows the difference between Ciribiribin and Tchaikovsky's Piano Concerto No. 1 is definitely a maverick plover, well, maybe. Ah huh, if ol' Rene Descartes could have read what I'm reading now from Michael

Dudley's *Man, Gods and Nature*[1] he might have thought twice before elevating man as the only thinker in the universe.

> "Migrating birds are some of the most extraordinary thinking animals. Flying thousands of miles— sometimes, like the plover, over open ocean with no navigational cues but the sun and stars—they make their expected landfall, often returning to the same branch of the same tree year after year. Although storms may force migrating birds hundreds of miles off course, their compensating navigational ability allows most to reach their intended destination."

Or professor Stephen T. Emlen of Cornell University, who used indigo buntings (which are night migrants) to show that these birds depended on stars in the northern part of the sky, and that they need not see all of them in order to orient successfully.

He showed—

> ". . .their ability was acquired, not inborn. At first, young buntings determined the north-south axis by rotation of the stars, but soon learned to determine direction by star patterns."

Back to Dr. Dudley:

> "Birds have some sensory powers that far exceed man's: their vision is acute; some see polarized and ultraviolet light as well as color; some hear

---

1   Na Kana O Ka Malo Press, Honolulu, Hawaii 1990

infrasound—noise in ultralow frequencies of long wavelength that may carry for a thousand miles or more in the atmosphere; and some sense the earth's magnetic field and read direction by that sense."

I can't speak for Monsieur Descartes, but I ain't never met no *Homo sapiens* that could do all that.

I will, from this time forward, take the expression, "Dis is for da birds" as a supreme compliment for my fellow (and perhaps, superior) thinkers.

Henry and I continue a very pleasant relationship, albeit very formal. I suspect he senses my new respect, bordering on awe, and is a little tired of my observing and jotting down his every flutter. Nevertheless, I feed him three times a day, on a plate of course, replenish his bath with fresh water, and jointly attend our morning and newly added afternoon symphony concerts by the Pacific.

He continues to enjoy his ten-foot-square homestead on the hill, sunbathing mostly and looking out to sea as if searching for a sign known only to his kind. On rare occasions, he will peck at the screen door; I'll let him in and he'll prance for a bit, chase John Muir off the windowsill, and finally light down on my aging *New World Dictionary* for a nap.

I stare at him for hours at a time. It's a paralyzing wonderment that comes over you when you're in the presence of a great achiever. They're from another world, a magical world where impossible things are merely part of their routine. Things you can only dream about but never touch. This three-pound miracle of evolution placidly snoozing a few inches from me routinely takes on gale force winds, raging seas, and torrential rains on a

5,000-mile odyssey with nothing more than a calm faith in his ability to read the stars and land on the head of a pin in the middle of the world's largest ocean.

I'm in the presence of a peak performer and I've got that feeling again. It's the same one I felt when I was standing next to my Uncle Al, the clubhouse security guard at Ebbets Field in Brooklyn when Jackie Robinson walked by, patted me on the head, and said, "Hi, kid." Aside from watching my dad win a medal for being Fireman of the Month in New York City, it was the first time I was that close to greatness. And when immortality pats you on the head, you remember everything about that moment . . . his pigeon-toed walk, the sweat stains on the peak of his cap, the clump of grass clinging to the heel of his right spiked shoe, and the smile that seemed to be looking deep down inside you. Your eyes are under strict orders from your memory to take in everything.

Jackie was a giant . . . so is Henry.

I'm not quite sure he's one of those magnificently brilliant plovers or not, but I'm telling myself he is. I guess I just need to feel I'm back in the company of heroes.

20

"Have You Ever Wanted to Walk Naked in the Rain?"

Of course you have. It's a common compulsion of our species, like wanting to yell every time you drive through a tunnel so you can hear your echo. Right?

Well, it's raining and I've got that feeling.

It's August 17, 3:10 in the morning. Can't sleep. Cup of tea. Sit on the porch and look at the night. Maui lights still flickering on the horizon. Easy breeze shuffling in from the south barely causes movement in the tree of life. The ever-present rapid-transit clouds are in the slow lane tonight, content to circle a three-quarter moon and go nowhere. I have no agenda. No direction. No obstacles. No needs. I'm beyond alpha. That same state of peaceful nothingness you get when you stare into a campfire. I am a modern man in a treehouse at the edge of Eden, finally at one with simplicity.

A light rain falls, adding a soft touch of violins to my moonlight sonata.

The common compulsion speaks, "Get naked and walk to the water's edge." I do.

Suddenly it's Genesis and I'm Adam in the first garden—free, innocent, and open to every sensual joy in nature. I'm fifty plus. I've swum in a cool country swimming hole on a hot summer's day. I've hit a bases-clearing double in the big game. I've jumped from airplanes and floated through moist clouds of spring. I've climbed a mountain or two, and I've stood on the forecastle of a battle wagon, taking the spray from all five oceans. I've loved and been loved.

All have been great teachers of what's really important in life.

But to walk naked in a summer night's rain is to feel the wonder of a new birth. Truly, it's that good. I AM NATURE! I am a part of all that surrounds me. I am in harmony with something greater than my own intelligence. What I've known before, I can now feel. And without feeling, all the books of metaphysics are as useless as poetry to a drowning man.

I sing. I tumble and spread eagle on the wet grass. The most nourishing liquid in the cosmos dances on my every pore. Talk about being refreshed . . . WOW!

An old Molokai tale has it that, if you need an answer, listen to the ocean at night. You'll get the right one. I listen. And I do get a message.

The Pacific sounds strangely like my mother tonight:

"You'll catch double pneumonia, nature boy, if you don't get your wet tush back in that treehouse, *now!*"

Ah, Ma, I'm a kid and I want to play. I walk up and down Omaha Beach doing a tropical rendition of Gene Kelly's "Singing in the Rain" dance followed by Jimmy

Durante's "Inka Dinka Doo." Show's over. Back on the two-lane in front of the treehouse. Arms extended, face to the heavens for one final rapture. Absurdity once again comes calling.

Three olive-drab military jeeps, one half-track truck carrying various implements of destruction, and one truckload of helmet-clad soldiers splashes by in rapid succession. I'm hit with a half dozen flashlights and a barrage of catcalls, jeers, and a final humiliation in the form of an old local drinking song, "Ain't no beeg ting, bruddah."

Who's invading Molokai at 3:40 in the morning?

Next day's *Molokai Dispatch* headlines tells who:

"Hawaii National Guard Conducts Nighttime Exercises On East End. Local Residents Outraged."

I'll say. I should have listened to my mother.

21

Aphrodite in Day-Glo

Morning fast walk into the sunrise.

I'm lighter on my feet. No aches and pains. Stamina is back.

Molokai magic.

On and on, past nature's finest jewelry, rich red anthuriums, night blooming Cereus, sunset bougainvillea, ironwood hedges, prized vanda orchids, and now a long stretch of the ancient medicinal plant, "the wand of heaven," aloe vera—now being romanticized by the profiteering cosmetic hucksters as a cure-all for everything from cellulite to crow's feet. Wait until they find out the Hawaiians have been using aloe for fourteen centuries to keep themselves "regular" and to help make babies.

There is solid folklore to substantiate both. Mr. Buelli, the gardener, told me. He's seventy-seven, has nine kids, and is very proud of the fact he never had a "problem."

Suddenly, the last island has a goddess—Aphrodite in an orange and green, skin-tight day-glo aerobics outfit, cut off at the thighs, about a quarter mile ahead, jogging toward me.

The fact is more dramatic than fantasy, for she literally appeared out of a lazy ground mist on a hill like one of those flaxen heroines from a Sappho sonnet. She has an Olympian's body: tall, taut, stunningly muscled, but not to distraction. Her substantial feminine assets are doing all the distracting.

Nothing is hidden.

Every ripple and roll of a muscle group bursts through that mercifully revealing outfit and keeps me a focused connoisseur of the moment. Her breasts are large and firm and threatening to escape their confines any moment.

Closer and closer.

The face is cover girl perfect. Deep blue eyes accentuating a mahogany tanned skin glistening in perspiration.

She's close, very close now. I can see the entire outline of her navel. She smiles. I'm not sure I return it. I'm inert except for a few raging hormones playing ping-pong with my nerve endings.

Without missing a stride, she looks back at the rising sun over her left shoulder and offers, "Gonna be a hot one today."

I can hear my libido shouting, "Can't imagine it getting any hotter than this."

My mouth responds with the kind of brilliant remark carefully designed to entwine our lives forever, "Yeah, but it's a dry heat."

She smiles again and jogs off through the thinning mist on the next hill.

My brush with living mythology is over. But I think I stand and stare for a very long time. When you're fifty, you want to hold onto euphoria as long as you can. You have every reason to doubt it will ever happen again.

"She leeves in one of does vacation cottage down da beach."

The voice with the crackling lilt belongs to an old Hawaiian gentleman in a Santa Claus beard standing a few feet away at the waterline. He wears the contented smile of a beachcomber and little else, except for his skimpy malo (Hawaiian loincloth).

I knew it. I've just walked into a Fellini daydream.

He's gathering shells and totally at home in his natural state. He punctuates every sentence with machine-gun-like cackle.

"Pretty woo-man. Training for da try-a-lon (triathalon). Comes here every summer. Runs na-kad at night. You like shells? He, he, he, he."

"Yes. What time? Where?"

"What time, what, where? He, he, he, he."

"What time and where does she run naked?"

"Diff-rent times, I think. Late, down dere," pointing to the long stretch of beach behind me.

My God, that's Omaha Beach! You mean every night while I've been cleansing my soul by candlelight with Mencken, Twain, Emerson, and Cardinal Neuman, the most structurally perfect female anatomy in the South Pacific is doing wind sprints in the buff on my front lawn?!

Starting tonight I schedule my cleansing during daylight hours.

The Laughing Seashell Man and I sit on a piece of driftwood. John Muir reclines in a fallen palm frond nearby.

In the days and weeks ahead this scene becomes a ritual. The script never varies. He talks about shells. I listen. John Muir sleeps.

He never volunteers his name, where he lives, or why he spends all his time searching for shells. I never ask.

He's an excellent teacher, demanding I repeat the colorful names of each new gem of the sea—the common harp, bubble conch, old woman triton, red-throated frog, marlin-spike auger, and seventy-two varieties of the ubiquitous shiny cowry. He knows them all.

This first day I break what will become an established routine and ask a question.

"What do you do with all these shells?"

He seems perplexed, pauses, and replies.

"Do? Why nut-ting. You don't *do* any-ting wit seashells. You jest. . ." Again he pauses, this time to reach for the right words. He finds them and continues, ". . .borrow da beau-tee for a little while and move on. He, he, he, he."

A few yards away on the narrow two-lane blacktop that runs the southern edge of the island a late model blue import car screeches around a hairpin turn at high speed and comes dangerously close to plunging into the rocky shoreline below. Two of the three occupants are terrified, a young native girl and a small child. The third, an older local female is unconcerned and floors the gas pedal out of the turn and speeds off toward town.

Without looking up, The Laughing Seashell Man mutters, "Pupule wahine (crazy woman). Same ting, three, four times a day. She got da mainland sickness."

"What's that?" I ask.

"Always rushing to nowhere." Then he adds, matter-of-factly, "She gonna die soon."

He leaves, but not before carefully replacing each shell back at the waterline.

John Muir and I, still separated by his three-yard margin of tolerance, watch a perfectly formed rainbow bridge east and west Maui across the channel.

Back toward the treehouse for a day of reading.

I've reached an easy certitude on one issue. If you're going to read the classic thinkers, read them only in the woods. No place else. All great universal truths were born in nature through observation. Taking an idea back to its birthplace somehow gives it a life it never had anywhere else. To read in the city is to merely process information, but to read by a crystal spring, alongside a fallen oak, or within smelling distance of a eucalyptus grove is to *feel* the utter simplicity of the human option in all good writing—be kind, help others, laugh a lot, preserve the flow of the planet, realize you're temporary, and follow your bliss. Everything else is satire.

Today I sit in the middle of the overgrown ruins of the Moanui Sugar Mill a few hundred feet above Omaha Beach. I'm reading to John Muir. Today it's Emerson's riveting poetic plea for self-esteem and independence of character, *Self Reliance*.

John does what he always does when I read to him. He lies on his right side and yawns a lot. Occasionally, not often, he will suddenly sit up and look me right in the eye.

I figure he's reacting to ancient pieces of truth cats throughout history have always known. I've made a point of marking those passages. One day I'll go back and look at them. Maybe I'll write a book—*The Wisdom of Cats*. A terrifying thought for someone who has been a dog man all his life.

Today, John jumps up and listens to this:

"Man is timid and apologetic; he is no longer upright; he dares not say 'I think, I am,' but quotes some saint or sage. He is ashamed before the blade of grass or the blowing rose. These roses under my window make no reference to former roses or to better ones; they are for what they are; they exist with God today. There is no time to them. There is simply the rose; it is perfect in every moment of its existence. Before a leaf-bud has burst, its whole life acts; in the full-blown flower there is no more, in the leaf-less root there is no less. Its nature is satisfied, and it satisfies nature, in all moments alike. But man postpones or remembers: he does not live in the present, but with reverted eye laments the past, or, heedless of the riches that surround him, stands on tiptoe to foresee the future. He cannot be happy and strong until he, too, lives with nature in the present, above time."

Nightfall. More reading. Finish my "b" and "c" words in the dictionary. I'm particularly taken by the Greek derivative noun "cacodemon," an evil spirit or devil, sometimes personified in a cat.

Can't deny the delectable image of Aphrodite in semi-see-thru day-glo is still with me.

So is the temptation to debunk the myth of her nocturnal nakedness. But alas, I came to the woods to enrich the spirit, not to bow to the flesh. Besides, my last brush with fantasy cost me a good chunk of self-esteem, not to mention a brand new pair of underwear.

I will not waver again.

22

Afloat on an Island

I waver.

A man in a treehouse does not live by reading and quiet contemplation alone. Primordial lust drives me to the water's edge . . . four nights in a row.

There's a problem. Nowhere to hide. Evening tide reduces the width of the beach to less than four feet, and thick vegetation abutting the shoreline makes concealment impossible. What to do?

Only one option left.

So, here I kneel in three feet of water, thirty yards off shore with bluing lips from the "Maui Express," a chilling wind whipping around the east end of the island, reminding me once again of the basic absurdity of all human behavior.

I've picked different times each night to cover all possibilities, but so far the myth has not become reality.

I can't hold out much longer. My skin below the waterline looks like an explosion in a prune Danish factory. I'm shrinking. I sing. I hum and otherwise pass the time watching John Muir stealthily creeping along a nearby seawall in search of an edible nightcrawler.

Like all quadrupeds, John, you're a realist. You accept what is. You smell. You touch. You taste. You see. You hear and you act on the fact. It's only we foolish bipeds, waist high in shivering hope, who'd rather wallow in fantasy than flourish in reality. Maybe you're right in keeping your distance from me. I've got nothing of value to teach you.

Ah, John, but the pursuit of fantasy does have its rewards.

Look at this magnificent moment. Look at those streaking silver-blue billowy clouds racing across that brilliant moon shooting a thousand beams of light across the Pacific, like Thor hurling fiery thunderbolts to earth. Look at it. There's enough candlepower bouncing off those waves to light up the Astrodome for a double-header.

And listen, John. Listen to the music of an infallible composer, the heave and sigh of ten-foot waves doubling their fists and pounding the coral heads behind us.

And willya look at those stars in the August heavens? You could navigate all the oceans, anchor south of the Antarctic Circle, stand at the center of all the world's advertised mystical geography from Stonehenge at midnight, the Jebel Musa, "Mountain of Moses," in the granite wilderness of south Sinai, and the central Sahara at the summer solstice . . . and never hear the song of divinity any purer than on one clear Hawaiian night.

A long pause just to feel this improbable moment— John Muir, the relentless hunter, has his prey. Hard to make it out at this distance. He stops halfway back across the seawall and gives me one of those aloof catty looks.

I hate it when he does that.

Okay, Mister Realist, maybe the wood nymph won't come gamboling through the moonbeams. So what! Sometimes just the anticipation of ecstasy is enough to fire a neutral soul. Maybe it's everything. Remember when you were a kid, the actual arrival of Christmas Day was a dry and disappointing thing.

A tragedy of sorts.

It meant the end of creating possibilities for wonder. It meant the end of what Christmas is all about—waiting for joy. We perfected the skill so young but learned the lesson so late.

It's all about what you do while you're waiting. Creating adventure by keeping expectation alive. That's why I called a "time out" from big city pursuits and took up residence in a treehouse. I want the thrill of waiting for Christmas again.

All right, I know, I know. It's not quite like running the rapids on the upper Amazon or snowshoeing through the Kurdistan in late November, but it's the same search to discover expectation, nurture it, and bring adventure back in your life. So lighten up, John, willya!

What am I doing, talking to a cat?! A stone-faced realist at that. What good is it? All you can see is a shriveled, half-naked, middle-aged voyeur slowly sinking into the spongy off-shore clay of the continental shelf. Had you the slightest tug of romanticism, you'd know I'm a Meistersinger waiting for the first sign of spring, Gauguin dreaming of his next model, Quixote anticipating a smile from fair Dulcinea.

I am optimism unbound!

John could care less. He sits and eats, stopping only to raise his head to catch the cool spray from the incoming wave.

I swim out to the breakers where the coral reef effortlessly halts the advance of curling thunder and instantly tames the anger of the Pacific.

I float on my back and catch the cooling spray of the incoming waves.

Afloat on an island.

At one with the flow of the tide. Resisting nothing. Being nothing. Feeling everything. The mighty trades dancing through my chest hair; the chatter of the shoreline palms; moonlight painting broad strokes across the latitudes; the leaping fish and land critters preparing to call it a day; the magic of nightfall tempering the distant flickering lights of Maui's self-destructive contract with commercialism; the eerie bellow of a breeching humpback like some medieval call to vespers; those living sapphires, the constellations, all at arm's length; Einstein, Newton, Ptolemy, Copernicus, Khayyam, and all the other eloquent star wanderers—their works still bouncing around out there, sending back calming reassurance from what Shakespeare called "the majestical roof fretted with golden fire"; peace, air, ether, contentment at the base of being; and the insignificance of every other rhythm but this one . . . nature on track. Forget your stress management seminars, abandon your wise men and their chants. Get on your back and float under a Pacific moon! Heal thyself. 'Tis the therapy of Titans.

How long did I travel in this weightless flight around the universe? A minute, a month, a century, I don't know.

I do know when I crash-landed.

Up on the road, the screeching of high-speed rubber twisting on concrete is reverberating through the valleys.

It's the "pupule wahine" taking the hairpins on two wheels and a full throttle. How can anyone be that angry in the middle of all this blessed beauty? I guess the Laughing Seashell Man was right. She's got "the mainland sickness."

Ah, one last look at this grand architecture, and then it's time to end this salty vigil and return to a life of modest self-denial (I'm getting low on sesame spaghetti).

Wait a minute! There is something moving on the beach a few hundred yards to my left. Can it be? No, this was just a midsummer night's dream from the start. These things only happen in those post-WW II French films. I never really expected—but there is someone running at the water's edge. My God! It is Aphrodite in Day-Glo—without the day-glo! Even at this distance I can recognize the century's greatest female shape in its entire flesh. Hooray! Dreams do come true in blue Hawaii. Now what? Gotta get closer—apparitions must be verified. How? Do I run the quarter mile in to shore and risk grinding my feet into poi on the treacherous coral, or do I try to break the world's record in the 440-yard individual freestyle and risk arriving late for the rendezvous with a deity? I opt for the Olympic gold. Wait a minute . . . wouldn't it be appropriate to meet the galloping goddess in a likewise natural state? I'm sure Bullfinch[1] would approve. Off with my faded yellow

---

1   Author of *Bullfinch's Mythology*

trunks with the illegible Burbank YMCA seal on the right leg. I'm on my way to immortality . . . or at least the thrill of a lifetime.

I'm on target for the gold, kicking and pulling at full speed and slicing through the silty water with ease. Incredible what a date with a naked woman will do for your breast stroke. I can feel all my hormones applauding the effort.

Not good enough. She's faster; almost dead ahead on the beach about fifty yards. Never make it. Better stop, look, and dream about what could have been.

The moon is my ally. It's following her like a giant spotlight as her world class body sprints at the water's edge, churning up a string of rooster tails in its wake.

The gossamer is rising. The apparition is clearer, much clearer. I must not forget this moment. Study the details. The long blond hair flowing straight back, separating into two golden wings. The straining thighs, the swelling biceps pumping the power to pull her faster and faster, the large perfectly rounded breasts dutifully pointed forward cutting the wind, kissing the spray, and waving ever so slightly from side to side in a sensuous ballet that brings me to my knees in appreciation.

She's slowing down. Why? Now she's stopping right in front of me. Perhaps the goddess has spied one of her adoring subjects and will summon him forth for an audience.

Wrong.

She bends down and is . . . petting . . . a cat! It's John Muir! That furry little Lothario got there first and is actually nuzzling the incredibly beautiful leg of a goddess. Oh my God, the little phony is doing his poor, pathetic

Oliver Twist act for her, and she's falling for it. Now she's picking him up and—I don't believe this—she cuddling the rat chaser close to those gorgeous twin guardians of that fabulous valley of untold pleasure.

Muir, you have no right to be in my fantasy again. You will never get another drop of milk as long as I'm halfway up a tree, so help me, H.L. Mencken.

She cuddles, she strokes, and then gently puts that smug little realist back down on the sand and flies off into the darkness around the bend. I will never see her again.

Back on shore Muir shortens our tolerance distance to two yards. I'm not buying it. I walk right by him, but not before looking him smack in those squinty emerald eyes and delivering my very best Bronx cheer.

I've been told by fanciers who know about these sordid things that it's not possible, but I had two yards and the benefit of moonlight, and I would be willing to swear . . . John Muir was smiling.

Maybe reality is not so overrated after all.

23

The Dying Season Is Here

Sunrise.

A strange stillness. The world has changed. The signs are everywhere. No wind. Can't be. This is the east end of Molokai, the fertile crescent, the one jewel in the archipelago that the goddess Hina, wife of Wakea, the ancestor of all Hawaiians, decreed would always receive the "breath of heaven."

Why not today?

A look at the "tree of life" tells the story.

The leaves are suddenly pale. The branches sag and you can hardly hear the giant breathe. And where's the morning chorus? There isn't any. The great hall is empty. The birds are gone and so are the mangoes. Not one left on the boughs or on the ground.

Can bark look sullen?

If cats can smile, then surely trees can feel sad.

Nature is recycling.

The great god Lono came during the night and declared the season of harvest is over.

So is my morning comedy theater. The Flying Santinis are gone. So is Donaghy and his looney tunes family. Nomadic consumers, they follow the crops. And starting today they're elsewhere. Only John Muir remains. His food chain has no seasons.

In the several weeks I witnessed the blooming of my one acre of Eden, hundreds of mangoes fell from this tree. Elsewhere, breadfruit, liliko'i (passion fruit), tangerines, bananas, grapefruit, a dozen varieties of berries along with limes, guavas, papayas, and coconuts ripened, lingered, and shriveled by the bushel!

A gaggle of swarthy fifty-year-old dropouts could happily thrive in the full blush of health on this nutritious windfall for all time. And this is just one of 4.1 million rich acres in just one tiny island chain.

I'm getting cosmic.

I'm beginning to believe it may be a crime against humanity just to focus without acting on the fact that 700 million people are going undernourished and hungry every day.

Life in the woods teaches you quickly that abundance is not a myth. That economic systems, not scarcity, create world hunger.

John Muir is sitting a yard and a half from his milk tin. Definitely not two yards. I know two yards when I see it, and this ain't it. Can it be that tolerance will soon turn to fraternity? I doubt it. I'm a lifelong dog man.

I begin pouring some 2% low-fat when a familiar screech ends with an unfamiliar piercing thud and pop. John and I head down to the two-lane. The smell of gasoline is heavy in the air.

A white pickup truck is lying on its side. A blue import is facing it head-on, accordioned to half its length. The pickup driver is shaken but miraculously unhurt. A neighboring farmer on horseback dismounts and places his finger on the neck of the blue import driver. It's the "pupule wahine." She's motionless, slumped across the wheel. Her commitment to anger is still frozen on her face.

The farmer nods and speaks in that unemotional, accepting way all farmers speak.

"She's maki (dead)."

The "mainland sickness" is a fatal disease.

24

"Thy Kingdom Come, Thy Nudge Be Done. . ."

How many times did you hear yourself saying, "I'm going to take a day for myself and do absolutely nothing." You usually wind up doing absolutely lots, like watching, thinking, worrying, sleeping, fantasizing, avoiding, mowing, and tinkering.

All of which is something.

We just can't seem to do what teenagers and practitioners of Zen seem to be able to do with relative ease—achieve a state of "nothingness." Brain shutdown. Move only when a much deeper voice equidistant from the heart and the gut fires the starter's gun.

I've always been a firm believer that there's a "beast voice," an inner nudging going on, pushing us in the direction our true talents want to be moving.

When the final history is written, I'm sure there'll be an asterisk next to "free will" with the explanation:

* In order to assure humans they were slightly different than paramecia, monkeys, and chrysanthemums, it was necessary to tell them they had this wonderful power to make whatever choice they wanted.

The fact is, they were all given one body, one soul, and one NUDGER. The latter, while the principal determinant of behavior, would allow the "will" to take all the credit for the sake of sound. Sound?

Sure. "Will" sounds better than "nudge." How would it sound to say, "Where there's a nudge, there's a way," or "Thy kingdom come, thy nudge be done." Textbook writers and religionists would never buy it. And doctors would never be able to keep a straight face when they looked their critical patients in the eye and intoned, "I've done all I can for you. Now it's up to you. You've got to have the nudge to survive."

In keeping with that spirit, we simply let "free will" get all the PR while "nudging" did all the work.

Today is graduation day!

Time to put the lesson of nature to work—go with the flow. Today I'm going to by-pass the brain and take all my orders from the nudger. It'll be up to the raw animal instinct to press the buttons.

What am I in for? A glimpse of the Beatific Vision or three to five with six months off for good behavior? What? How much of what I do is "them" and their ideas? You know them—the teachers, the priests, role models, mommy and daddy, the script writers—them. And how much of what I do is really me? And what happens when I do what the deep down me wants to do?

It's the biggest risk a fifty-year-old man can take. I'm excited and I'm sweating.

Will I start parking in the restricted handicapped-only areas? Will I graduate from being a closet aficionado of the ladies' underwear ads in *Woman's Day* and go up to strange females on the street and tell them how much I admire their body parts?

Or worse yet, will I discover that, deep down, we're all children of the dark, repressed looters and graffiti scrawlers, drive-by shooters of one sort or another just waiting to pounce upon the carcass of goodness when the lights are turned off? Is it care or fear that keeps us from running a red light late at night when no one is around?

Today I'll find out, maybe.

Being this is a diary, a ship's log of one voyage, I am restricted to being a mere recorder, not an editorialist. So, no erasures, no changes. Whatever happens, I'll write it down. No syntax, no structure. Let's make it a grammatical adventure as well.

Here goes.

8:10 a.m.

Load up my orange knapsack with pen, paper, a tape recorder, a camera, and a bottle of Pepto Bismol. Mom insisted we take it on all adventures . . . wait a minute . . . Mom is "them" . . . what does the nudger say . . . pause . . . hard to tell on this one where Mom leaves off and the nudge begins . . . hell, I'll take the Pepto . . . down to Omaha Beach to listen to the Pacific and wait for the grand nudge . . . .

High gray-flannel overcast sky hiding the clouds . . . air has a light chill but tender, refreshing . . . shadows add character to a day . . . I wonder if there were any shadows in Eden? . . . low tide . . . never really understood how there could be a high and a low tide in the same body of water . . . where does the low tide water go and where does the high tide water come from? . . . Swell, I'm trying to rediscover the meaning of life and I don't even know where the tides come from? . . . why haven't I ever felt lonely out here . . . the voice that never fails is gone . . . can't hear a thing . . . keep waiting . . . hard to shut down the brain-works . . . it always wants to deliver demands, draw pictures, stuff you don't call for, but it's there . . . Dad dying, me holding his hand singing the first song he ever taught me, "Tattooed Lady," just to hold back the tears . . . why am I writing this? . . . why does anybody write? They're afraid of dying . . . got to hurry up and put down my visions, my life as it was and as I wanted it to be before I die . . . seeing it on paper tells me I was here, I saw things, I diagrammed the sentence, I created my own impressions . . . tourist boat out in the channel . . . we're all tourists, passing through . . . commentators, that's what we are . . . look at the show, jot down your observations, that's all, no more . . . Mother Teresa was right, it's all a mystery, think good, do good, stay thin, laugh at the devil . . . John Muir up on the road above me rubbing against a palm branch . . . am I thinking, or is all this nudging? Clear the mind . . . do like the Tibetan monks and hum the earth mantra, "O-U-Mmmm" . . . shit, I swallowed a fly.

9:10 a.m.

It hits . . . clear, simple . . . CLIMB A TREE . . . across the two-lane, up the "tree of life," up past the first two major forks in the double trunk to the last cradle capable of supporting a 198-pound nihilist, twenty, twenty-five feet up . . . sit, do nothing . . . mind tricks or truth? Air smells stronger, sweeter here . . . why does the world look so different twenty-five feet off the ground? . . . New perceptions, new knowledge . . . the gift looks magical and fragile at the same time . . . same feeling the astronauts must get when they see the great suspension, planet Earth, for what it is—a delicate link in infinity with no lifetime guarantee . . . twenty feet or twenty million light years . . . same distance same knowledge . . . kids are natural climbers . . . they knew it was a giant leap to a better place, above the ordinary where kids are supposed to be . . . they're right . . . there is magic halfway up a tree . . . nothing looks important down there . . . same feeling I got in the Navy when my ship was pulling out to sea leaving the "land troubles" behind . . . no traffic, no race for personal gain, no stop signs, no wasting precious lifetime searching in gray places for meaning . . . at sea, looking back to shore, ahead to the open water, or halfway up a tree . . . same thing, you see the whole picture, forget meaning, just accept what is . . . being in a plane is too impersonal, too far . . . you've got to be in a tree to feel real flight . . . rates right up there with floating on your back off the breakers in the moonlight . . .

10:23 a.m.

Another nudge—EAT A CREAM CHEESE AND JELLY SANDWICH, NOW! . . . I kind of was expecting a more weighty message than this . . . don't question the nudge! . . . haven't eaten cream cheese and jelly in forty years . . . off to the store, in Kauakakai . . . an eighteen-mile walk . . . at the Hunomuni Bridge, at the seventeen-mile marker, a Norman Rockwell painting comes alive . . . seven kids are jumping off the bridge in ye ole swimming hole . . . more of a dirty old mud pit with large chunks of jagged concrete lying dangerously below the surface line, but wide and deep enough to serve the purpose of fun . . . one by one the young faces of Molokai—Hawaiian, Chinese, Portuguese, Filipino, Japanese, and all the mixtures between—are having the time of their lives contorting like pretzels and falling dead weight into the black water . . . "What kind of diving is that?" . . . the Spanky MacFarland look-alike with the pearly Hawaiian-Japanese eyes speaks for the group, "Da world fa-mus Molokai Bomber," everybody makes the we're-number-one sign and lets out a war whoop that runs up the valley behind us and comes back with twice the gusto . . . "You like try, mistah?" . . . yeah, I would, but no trunks . . . "So what, dis is Molokai, go fo' it" . . . the nudger agrees . . . off with my pants, down to my white boxers, up on the bridge railing . . . Spanky explains, "You gotta wait fo' a car, den jump and make one beeg splash. If you heet da car, boom, you become a Molokai Bomber." "What happens if I hit the concrete?" The littlest rascal wearing his father's trunks lights up, "We bury you fo' free." All laugh . . . The Molokai Bomber is just the old Brooklyn belly whopper with a little more arm action . . . kids around the world all seem to play in the same sand-box. Different names, same fun . . . here comes a brown and yellow truck with an official seal of some kind on the door . . . get set, timing is critical . . . truck just entering the bridge. Go! High jump, grab the legs in a tuck position, pray I miss being impaled on a concrete stake, splat, blop, explosive entry, rooster tails everywhere, a dead moose falling from a hundred feet couldn't a done any better . . . I know I've made Brooklyn proud even as I sink a few feet in the slimy bottom of the hole . . . I pop up to a thunderous chorus of "Cheecken skeen![1]" and thumbs up. The truck is stopped a few feet away, black gooky water running down the windshield. I made it. I'm a Molokai Bomber! . . . the truck belongs to Maui Electric Company. The two local men inside are smiling. They know all about swimming hole hijinks . . . they get out and set up survey equipment . . . the kids suddenly become quiet watching them . . . they know. Everybody on the island knows Maui across the channel needs more power and wants to put up a big ugly power station on Molokai so it won't create an eyesore for the Maui tourists. The kids look at me and know I know, too . . . I get up on the railing and risk paying my health insurance deductible with another sensational Molokai Bomber. Bullseye number two all over the surveying sticks. The valley rings with laughter, strengthened I'm sure by the ancient gods who protect this special land . . . .

11:15 a.m.

Back on the road . . . underwear hanging on the outside of my pack drying in the unseasonable ninety-degree heat . . . prepared to walk sixteen more miles if I have to . . . I don't . . . the world's funniest-looking half-automobile, half-motorized trash can picks me up. It's the Hippie Lady and her little Mohawk son . . . I say, "Thank you."

---

1   Local pidgin expression meaning "Right on!"

She says, "What part of New York are you from?" I say, "Brooklyn." She says, "Small woild, me too." Can't be. Brooklyn had weirdos, con men, and phony balonies, but no hippies. She's got to be a transplant. Every hard "a" and "r" out of her mouth tells me she's not. I was unkind in my initial assessment of her. Nice lady. A schoolteacher who got tired of being shot at by heavy-metal Mongols and being told there's nothing she can do about it went to the woods to seek a better life. Met a disillusioned accountant from Phoenix named Seth and mated to produce Sam, the cherub-faced three-year-old with the Cochise haircut and a genuine sense of wonder about nature. She invites me to their "place" in the forest. My nudger says don't listen to that heavily biased eastern seaboard conscience that labeled all flower children in Viet Cong pajamas and rubber sandals a smelly androgynous rabble of left-wing loafers destined to live off the system they sought to destroy. I don't listen. Today my slate is clean. I'm a free man.

Their place, like life itself, should not be judged on first impression. An acre of mini-clearings, each filled with the primitive but functional tools of wilderness survival and linked by a rather substantial, rock-lined pathway. It's what you might see in a museum's historical diorama of an early "Pioneer Family Encampment." Clean, spartan, respectful of the natural architecture around it.

The first clearing, about thirty yards off the road and walled in by eighty-foot kukui trees, is the "main house"—a ten-by-ten scrap plywood and fish netting shack reinforced by the strength of several felled giants. Inside, just the bare necessities—bed, chair, and a writing desk, all handmade. The disillusioned accountant "who never put a nail to hammer before" has learned to become an exceptional carpenter. Clothes are hung on outside hooks next to a modest open-air library containing one weather-beaten *Guide to Medicinal Herbs*, one rain-soaked *Encyclopedia of Edible Plants*, and one close-to-brand-new *King James Bible* carefully protected in cellophane.

In other clearings are showers, complete with hot water tanks, a cistern system modeled after the original Roman version, a kitchen with two earthen hearths, table and chairs made from forest lumber, and food shelves placed in the curve of the tree trunk. Off to the side, through the mini-wheat field, to the stream that runs all the way up to Mount Kamakou is a blooming garden of corn, tomatoes, and berries.

The lady leads little Sam into the underbrush, points out a big red blossom, carefully explains to him that it's called red ginger and can, and will, be used by them to make soap. He plucks it and examines it reverently, like a botanist with a rare find. He hands it to his mother. She squeezes its soft white substance over her arms and face. "It can also be used as a perfume. I'm teaching Sam to become friends with all of nature's gifts."

Young Sam has learned well. He darts around, through and over the natural landscape, with the agility of an African Bushman.

"Wanna see the enchanted forest?" Sam asks. He grabs my hand and takes me a few hundred yards further back through a natural trellis of keawe trees leading to a forest within the forest. Only this one has no relation to the other. Two immediately distinct worlds. My little Mohawk guide is right. Instant enchantment.

A swaying cathedral of giant eucalyptus trees, white and rain cloud gray, with huge serpentine tentacles where branches ought to be, thick, heavily veined muscled stalactites hanging like petrified waterfalls. A snow forest in the summertime. It's as if a giant hand had plucked the mangroves from Omaha Beach and hung them on the clouds. It is the foggy legendary magic of Merlin. A predawn rendezvous for the brave knights of the realm before battle.

Sam wants to know, "What does it look like to you?"

Thanks to the Witch Hazel Man, I'm learning to pause before I speak.

"Hmmmm, how about a mass gathering of multi-robed ecclesiastics extending their arms in a blessing. What do you see?"

"Just trees in a storybook." Another little realist.

They share their modest meal of broccoli bits, tomatoes, blueberries, and baked breadfruit with me.

What they need they make or grow or take from nature, that which nature willingly bestows. They don't take drugs or any chemically prepared foods. I asked them. They read to one another, laugh a lot, welcome the rain, and haven't had a headache or back pain since they gave up the hunt in the city and settled here.

I tell them how impressed I am with their rustic ingenuity. And I am. They beam with a farmer's modest pride. No money, no television, no electricity, no help, nothing but a smiling faith in independent living and the value of simplicity to give it all meaning.

They escort me to their "front door," a chopped-through opening in a keawe thicket.

I have one final question.

"Tell me why, of all the places in the world, did you choose Molokai?"

The Red Ginger Lady smiles, but it's the quiet Seth who answers, "Hard to explain, really. Sometimes you just hear a voice telling you what you really should do . . . and you do it."

"I think I know what you mean."

We shake hands, and I'm back on the road.

I will never label another human being again.

25

The "Field of Dreams" Is Not in Iowa. . .

The nudge continues. . .

12 Noon

Picked up at the fifteen-mile marker by the musical Kawili family in their rusting, belching, wobbly *Grapes of Wrath* '39 Chevy truck. Mom and Dad up front singing. Grandpa with an Al Capone-size cigar on ukulele. Four kids in the back with one goat, one lamb, one monster poi dog[1] with a pirate patch over his left eye, a box of live hard-shell crabs, two chewed-up surfboards shredding at the edges, a wheelbarrow without a wheel, mattresses, clothes, boxes of stuff. And now me.

The kids are shy. The goat isn't. He's eating my drying underpants. Breaks the ice. Laughter.

"Where you leeve, Uncle?"[2]

---

1   Mongrel
2   Island kids call male strangers with white hair "Uncle."

"In a tree."

More laughter. I'm accepted.

"Where you folks going?"

"Lookin' fo' some place to stay. We got keeked outta our house. No money fo' da rent."

Grandpa sticks his head through the back window.

"Any song requests from back dere?"

I ask for my favorite, "Kuni Au," King Kamehameha's drinking song. We all sing.

Sure it's an idyllic island. Sure the "aloha" is real and nobody starves. But what is it deep down these "have nots" have that allows them to face all adversity with a laugh and a community sing-along?

"Aren't you guys worried?" I ask.

The oldest kid, feeding the lamb his cherry popsicle, replies with a broad grin, "What fo'? We togettah."

More realism from a short person.

The goat is finished with my drawers and now tries a surfboard for dessert. Everyone seems content to let him enjoy his meal.

12:20 p.m.

Arrive at the Friendly Store Market. Buy one loaf of honey wheat bread and a pound of cream cheese and a giant-size jar of grape jelly . . . walk to the park opposite the senior citizens center on the outskirts of town . . . six old men sitting on the bench staring off into space. Doc Chu is the only one I recognize from the "Streetcar Named Delirious." We talk. They got bored and walked out of the community singing session and are waiting for their bus ride back home, where they'll do some more waiting.

I make seven sandwiches and distribute them to "the boys." We eat. We smile. We enjoy. It's obvious none of them have ever had this combo in their mouths before.

The Old Filipino Man with the rusty walker says, "Good, but too dry." So I buy a gallon of passion orange juice and we wet down the sandwiches.

I love old folks. They're where we're all heading. As far as I'm concerned, they are life's only valid outside consultants. I received my first sustained booing as a professional speaker many years ago when I suggested we replace all psychiatrists with a senior citizen in his chair and then watch the mental health of the nation improve. I was keynoting the American Psychiatric convention in Newport Beach, California, at the time. I'm very proud of that response.

We soon all agree singing "I've Been Working On The Railroad" is a big waste of their dwindling time. I make a suggestion. "How about a game of ball?"

Sudden silence. Strange looks. Old folks have no use for diplomacy. They ask me if I have brain damage.

I convince three of them to come out on the field with me and play a game with the laughing little leaguers already in the middle of a pick-up game.

A little practice first.

The kids relinquish their equipment to us and sit on the sidelines to see who drops dead first.

The Old Filipino Man with the walker goes to first; Doc Chu, the eighty-something retired dentist who didn't believe in anesthesia, adjusts his bottle-thick glasses and tries to find third base. I'm pitching and the Hawaiian Man with the lion's hair has thrown down his cane and picked up a bat.

Play ball!

First pitch and, whack! A soft liner in the hole. Doc Chu doesn't see it. He's still looking for third base. The little leaguers recognize courage when they see it and are running out to retrieve the balls and assist the "veterans."

Great feeling. Suddenly there's no such barrier called age. Everything is possible again.

Whack! Mr. Lion's Hair may be slightly paralyzed on the left side, but his right side remembers how to swing the wood. A dribbler to "Chico" Chu who gobbles it up thirty seconds after it comes to a dead stop at his feet. A surprisingly strong throw to first that takes two bounces and caroms off the top of Mr. Filipino's walker and . . . he catches it! Cheers all around. Both young and old appreciate instant achievement.

Mr. Filipino is beaming. He's found the little kid inside. Life is good again. The other three cream cheese eaters on the sidelines are feeling their testosterone and join us. And Molokai has its first ever "over-eighty" softball team.

Everybody gets a chance to hit. The Retired Chinese Cane Field Worker forgets what side of the plate he used to hit from but manages to rap a line drive down the left field line. "Chico" Chu requests that I pitch about five feet from home plate so he can see the ball. He also asks me to "shout out when the ball gets close." "Pee Wee" Matsumura, the Retired Ranch Hand, can't hold a bat. Rheumatoid arthritis. He uses his thick black cane to pop out to the Portuguese Ex-Airline Baggage Handler at short, who is gently led to the ball by two thoughtful little leaguers.

We end with a team yell (and a lot of coughing) and the world's record for the most errors committed by a team on Social Security.

"Pee Wee" is sick to his stomach. He says the cream cheese was stale. I offer him some of my Pepto. He waves it off and pulls out his own bottle from his black L.A. Raiders ditty bag. I'm sold. Don't go nudging without Pepto. The Old Filipino Man grabs my arm and takes me aside. He very seriously suggests, "Maybe we ought to start a league."

26

The Nudge Goes to Sea

The rest of my day on the winds of the inner voice is all about asking and getting . . . I want to get a row boat and row out to the breakers. I ask the first fisherman I see. He gives me his boat. I want to learn how to hold onto a sail connected to a surfboard and ride the wind over the waves. I shout out that intention to a dark-skinned wind-surfer flying by. He shouts back I should meet him on shore. I do, and he teaches. A half-hour later a friendly trade whips through the Maui-Lanai passage for just an instant, long enough to hurl me through the clouds into outer space beyond the wonders of time travel to another world—at one with the wave and the wind. It lets me down gently and disappears. I'm tired. I sleep on the beach. No idea how long I've slept. It feels good. Like the naps you take on the massage table.

The final nudge of the day leaps off the scale in degree of difficulty—go to sea! I don't mean in a rowboat. I mean in a ship of the line. I mean taking the spray off the bow plowing through the black and silver night in the middle of the channel, standing in the greatest site of adventure that ever was—the wheelhouse. I hear Jack London applauding. No suggestion as to how to accomplish the feat, just applauding. Ask all the boat owners at the pier if they'll take on a passenger tonight. No one is shipping out except the Leahi, a 125-ton ocean going tug. She's pulling a 240-foot-long barge filled with a few thousand tons of ripe watermelons, empty storage containers, and one Model T Ford bound for Honolulu, fifty nautical miles away.

Kolo the lanky Hawaiian stevedore says, "No way you gonna hitch a ride. Insurance, union problems, stuff like dat."

Kolo doesn't know the power of the nudge to cut through stuff to get things done.

Find the captain. He's on the forecastle, sitting on Teddy Roosevelt's mustache, the large corded bumper hanging over the prow, reading the paper. Now, you expect the commanding officer of a tug to have a name dripping with bilge water and covered in rusty anchor chains . . . a name like Horst or Bull or Jebodiah. But definitely not Dick.

He doesn't look like a Dick. He looks like a middle linebacker from hell. A fireplug with a beer belly the size of a grounded dirigible. Some people have character lines in their face. Captain Dick has gullies and craters. He's bigger than a bear, but smaller than a redwood. But not much. His smile is easy. He's a good giant with a cradle-rocking soft voice moving slowly through the half-inch gap in his front teeth and rolling effortlessly over his swollen lips.

"Cap'n, I'm not going to snow you. Today's my day for pulling stuff up from the gut raw and seeing what happens. I want to ride with you tonight on your run to Oahu. I'll sign a waiver releasing you and your company of any liability, anything you say. I've just got this tremendous urge to be under those stars tonight at sea. I'm a writer. Maybe the experience will find its way into a story somewhere in a magazine or book, but right now the only place I plan to stick it is in my diary. I'm an ex-Navy man, know my way around a deck, and would be willing to wipe off the engines if you want. Or I'll just keep out of your way altogether. I just need to feel some salt spray tonight."

His smile is slow, starting in the southern end of the gullies, defying gravity as it trickles upstream toward the exploding thicket where his eyebrows should have been.

He reads from the paper.

"Be a dreamer today. Stay close to nature. Update your résumé. Take a chance. Greater insight comes through an experience with a younger person."

He raises his massive head.

"My horoscope. I'm a Leo. How old are you?"

"I'm fifty-one. I'm a Gemini."

"I'm fifty-five. You're younger."

His smile slides comfortably into a full-blown laugh. It's the bellowing laugh of a giant. Stevedores on the pier look up.

We shake hands.

"We shove off at 2200 (10:00 p.m.)"

At Sea

All lines in. Engines ahead one third. Right standard rudder. Big Jake and Alu, the two-man crew, are aft at the giant windlass carefully feeding out the inch-and-a-half-thick wire umbilical cord to the 3,000-ton behemoth lumbering above and behind us. By the time we pass the sea buoy they've fed out 200 feet. Captain Leo the Lion munches on some Lorna Doone cookies as he brings the wheel right to 270 degrees as we parallel the southern coastline. His penetrating gaze is fixed on a routine. First dead ahead into the pitch-black night. Then to the radar off to the side, and then aft at the long tow line bouncing off the waves and disappearing into the night. By the time we're abeam of Man-On-The-Rock Point, Big Jake locks off the windlass and shouts up to the wheelhouse, "1,600 feet, Captain."

Captain Leo waves back.

I ask the obvious landlubber's question, "How come the barge is towed so far back, Captain?"

His lips barely move as he stays riveted on the radar scope. "Less strain. Lots of small fishing boats without lights out there tonight. Keep a sharp eye."

"Aye, aye, Captain."

Meaning, purpose, simplicity, direction. It's all here at sea. What more could modern man on hiatus ask for? Success means doing your job right now one nautical mile at a time. Take care of the process, and the end result will take care of itself.

Forty minutes we stand silent in the compact wheelhouse bathed in the subdued glow of red light. Standard for seagoing vessels at night. Helps to acclimate to the dark.

The name on the log book says Captain Richard Twelvetrees, but I know different. It's Wolf Larsen, Jack London's "Sea Wolf," a tortured soul married to the sea for reasons no landlocked dreamer could ever understand.

Suddenly Wolf breaks the silence with an unsolicited mini-autobiography.

"I'm a full-blooded Choctaw Indian from Muskogee, Oklahoma. Didn't see a body of water bigger than a bathtub until I was twenty-six. I was living with a woman in Las Cruces, New Mexico, in '63. Went away for three days, came back, and she was in bed with a merchant seaman. Wanted to kill him. Had a beer with him instead. Real nice guy. Convinced me to go to sea." Wolf didn't expect a reply. I didn't give him any.

More silence. A few more Lorna Doones and he offers, with noticeable pride, "Tugs supply ninety percent of the goods for all these islands."

Another long pause. He checks the stars and presents his last complete sentence of the cruise.

"It's good to know what you're doing means something."

Indeed.

Bright moon, light breeze, gentle sea, rolling five degrees port and starboard. As the flickering lights of Molokai fade off our starboard quarter, I get that old Navy feeling again—I'm at sea, none of those silly land monsters can get you, you know.

I walk out on the port flying bridge and catch a trade kicking up in the channel as we round La'au Point on course 290 degrees for Honolulu.

What a magnificent day! Started off halfway up a tree and ends under a bright moon, making ten knots with a following current.

A twenty-foot swell whacks us amidships and delivers a thick sheet of salt spray topside. I'm drenched. The Pacific is talking to me again—"The world is a refreshing place if you stick to your nudge."

27

Goodbye, John . . . I'll Miss You

4:10 a.m.

Strange sound wakes me up. Half whimper, half howl.

Living in a treehouse you learn to identify all the sounds of the night—the mongoose scampering in the tall grass, the axis deer foraging on the hillside, Mert and Marge heading off a cane field rat, coconuts falling on the wet sand, shifts in the wind across the Pacific, even the flutter of different birds, the harsh wap-wap of the mynah, the softer lullaby of the cardinal. I know them all. But this one is different. I'll ask Buelli tomorrow.

6:40 a.m.

I won't have to ask Buelli.

I open the screen door with my usual pie tin of 2% low fat and get my answer. It's John Muir, lying in a pool of blood, both flanks ripped open, torn vessels dangling, face and neck raked with deep gashes. From the size of the wounds, I'd say it had to be that black-and-white pit bull at the nineteen-mile marker. He must have been one or two steps quicker than John figured.

I touch my constant distant companion for the first time. The soft velvety fur still has the feel of life. Below it, the body is stiff, hard.

I wrap John in my "Keep Molokai Free" T-shirt and bury him a few feet up from the high water mark on Omaha Beach, site of his greatest triumph. Mert and Marge mosey over and join the impromptu ceremony.

"Well, folks, I'm not very good at this sort of thing. You see, I've been a dog man all my life. But here goes . . . here lies John Muir, a realist and the most ornery, independent, aloof critter I almost ever met in my entire life. We talked. We took long walks at dusk, even shared an adventure or two, but I can't say we were friends. We just sort of . . . accommodated one another. John was a lot closer to nature than I was, so maybe he knew that accommodation in the wilderness is about the best thing you can hope for. He taught me to accept things for what they are, not what I'd like them to be. That the best approach to the big questions—no, any questions—is the direct one, with no side trips to sentiment or fear. See it. Face it. Decide. Do it and move on."

At the east end of Omaha Beach, up a few yards from the high water mark under the shade of a rubbing palm frond, is a mound of red dirt mixed with the spongy white sand. Over it is an old pie tin for a headstone, a fresh gallon of 2% low-fat milk, and a slightly used copy of *Jack London in the South Seas*.

Aloha, John. I'll miss you.

28

God Speaks from the Rafters of the Living Door

A new sabbath. A new church. Up the coast two miles to services. Try to sneak by the Gospel Shoers, who started their congas and clapping early today. No luck. The canoe-paddling minister sticks his head out the window and, without missing a beat on his big Cuban drum, shouts out, "Morning, Bob. You joining us today?"

Truth is my shield.

"No, I'm Pentecostal today—Church of the Living Door."

He smiles the true smile of Christian fellowship and shouts back, "Nice people, but they don't sing as much as us."

Hallelujah for small blessings!

The Living Door has no front door and very few of the faithful. Just eight of us. Two of the ladies are bus mates on the "Streetcar Named Delirious," Aunty Tunee and Aunty Keala. We wave. We hug. We exchange aloha, Hawaiian style. We chat about arthritis, kidney failure, old men who sleep and dribble in church, how old-timers are getting greedy and selling the best land in Molokai to rich mainlanders, and laryngitis.

"Da min-istah no can speak," says Aunty Tunee.

"How come?" says I.

"He went to Honolulu to a speech class fo' to learn how to geeve bettah sermons, and he jes' speak himself outta his voice." Her laugh bounces off the walls and gets everybody smiling.

She grabs my arm. "Don't worry. We gonna have gud service anyway. No talking, jes' singing."

God help me.

I've been to twenty-three different churches on this small island, and every one of them shares an abiding love in the Lord, the aina, and light opera.

Aunty Keala walks to the first pew, gets a thought, stops, and shouts back at me.

"I taught you were a Methodist."

I shout back, "I was last week."

We sing. The minister sucks on a lemon.

A haole lady hands me a Hawaiian hymnal.

"Good morning. I'm Delma. Nice to see a new face." She is indeed. Sits down next to me, and in less time than it takes the minister to change the altar cloth, check with the organist on today's selection, and cut up another lemon, Delma Kahalawai has given me the highlights of her thirty-nine years of life.

Her story is right out of a romance novella. Southern California beauty queen destined to meet and marry a young handsome business genius who will provide her with a lifetime supply of platinum credit cards and a chalet in the Alps, instead falls madly in love with a visiting dark-skinned Hawaiian hula dancer at a church social. Marriage, four keikis, and life below the poverty level. Back to his native Molokai where he can be close to the things he knows best: fishing, hunting, and herding cows. She loves her family. She goes and makes do.

All through the singing, sign-language service we exchange glances. Not the glance of would-be lovers, but the glance of a missionary in the outback who meets a traveling salesman from her hometown and yearns to talk about familiar things. At least that's what I'm reading as I'm bringing in the sheaves. Delma is no longer a pretty woman, but the suggestions of former beauty are still alive. The deep blue eyes overpower the dark shadows around them and continue to sparkle. Beneath her farm-simple cloth dress is a body still curved to arouse desire. She has the kind of attractiveness men call handsome when they don't know how to describe it. Her lips are parched and the hair has long ago lost its luster, but her smile still carries a spark of passion that teases your imagination.

The chubby organist with the white hibiscus in her hair stands and announces she's just filling in for Minnie, the regular organist off visiting her brother-in-law on dialysis in Tupelo, Mississippi. She'll just play chords. Unfortunately, most of them are the wrong ones. But it doesn't matter to this genuinely happy, caring bunch of worshipping Hawaiians who all seem genetically able to cope with any human being's shortcomings. As long as you smile, keep a positive thought, and understand humility is more important than position, you can easily be accepted.

Suddenly, the second-string organist jumps up and announces, "One of his kidneys is doing gud. Da utter is in trouble. Please keep his bad kidney in your prayers. Also, my husband and my boys couldn't be here today. They're paddling in the big canoe race to Lanai. Please keep them in your prayers."

Aunty Keala wants to add to our prayer list. She adjusts her hearing aid and shouts with the vigor of a jet engine backfiring. "Don't forget Moses Kekapono. He's got can-sah of da prostate. Also pray for da minis-tah's voice fo' to return."

Aunty Tunee gives her a good-natured poke to the rib cage and declares with equal volume, "No, don't pray fo' dat. His larin-gitis is da answer to *my* prayers."

The house of the Lord bellows with laughter, as it does every Sunday in every church on this island. The local people unashamedly give their religions what religions desperately need in tough times—fun, the power to see humanity for the unimportant thing it really is.

The lemon-sucking minister is convulsed in silent laughter. Delma has her hand over her mouth to stifle a positive emotion the way embarrassed country ladies sometimes do.

I've never really been very comfortable sitting in a church that relentlessly shouts life should be a joyful celebration but insists on painting its windows and decorating its house with the most bloody, maudlin scenes of pain in its history. When are the Christian interior designers going to lighten up and paint big smiles on the faces of the holy men and women of the Bible? After all, they're announcing "Good news"! I'm tired of feeling sorrow, not joy. Guilt, not giddiness. No more. Molokai is changing all that. I've always felt closer to God when I was laughing out loud. Right now, I'm close.

The man with the impish grin in the first pew is giving the sermon for the silent minister. He tries to make eye contact with the congregation. He can't. They're all looking elsewhere. A bewildered bluejay has wandered into the house of the Living Door and is struggling to find its way back out into the world of the flesh and the devil. My, how it struggles. Flying full speed into deceptively clear window panes hoping for a quick escape route. Up to the rafters. A mad dash to the altar. A sudden hop to the shoulder of Jesus on the crucifix. A jittery, twitchy wait for inspiration, then a direct flight to the American flag.

Mr. Impish Grin is delivering a very powerful message based on Luke 7:36-50—Jesus accepts a dinner invitation from a Pharisee and speaks His mind. Our surrogate minister is interpreting the story to mean we all need to be more open and honest in our face-to-face communications.

No one is listening.

All eyes remain on Mr. Bluejay's kamikaze dives into the big stained glass window behind the altar.

All eyes but mine. Delma's modest blue-white dress is responding to the simple laws of physics and has inched up well over her knees as she squirms in her pew over the plight of the bird. I'm beginning to reassess the salesman and the missionary relationship.

She feels my gaze, turns, and physically exposes another inch of some very attractive legs. This new angle also opens the crossover flap on her bodice, revealing a flimsy bra doing very little to hide her fruitful bounty.

Delma is showing all the signs of a quiet sexuality sizzling under a sultry calm.

Our eyes meet, and there's no hiding the message. We're face to face, open and communicating. But, I'm sure this is not what Luke 7:36 had in mind.

We smile that awkward "maybe" smile. The one that sends the "what if" message. Now, I'm back to feeling guilty. I'm sinning grievously in thought. I see our sweating naked bodies writhing in ecstasy, bathed in soft moonlight on the front lawn of the treehouse. I know the same slow-motion film is playing on her imaginary screen. The frustrated housewife, displaced from things that might have been, and the gray-haired stranger in the Molokai Taro Patch T-shirt, bravely sailing through a mid-life crisis relapse.

Our pot is boiling over.

And lust has blinded me to Mr. Bluejay's latest position. He's perched on the rafter directly over my head. How does a guilt-ridden sinner with super-charged hormones know that? Because Mr. Bluebird's neurotic frenzy has peaked. He's lost all bodily control and sends an airmail special delivery brushing my forehead and splattering the lower left side of my Hawaiian Hymnal, song 146, "Ka-haku-no-ku'u Pu'uhonua," and the front of my T-shirt. So much for passion in the pew.

Laughter returns to the house of the Lord, loud and long. The sudden burst of emotion sends Mr. Bluejay scurrying again. This time he finds an open jalousie and is free at last.

I stand to an enthusiastic applause.

"I was expecting a message from on high when I came here but this isn't it."

Aunty Tunee shouts, "Maybe it is."

More laughter.

I have seen one-of-a-kind sunsets, sunrises, and rainbows. I've heard the Pacific talk and the wind play Mozart, but never was the voice of the Almighty so loud . . . or His aim more accurate.

Hallelujah! One lifelong search is over. God does have a sense of humor.

My faith is getting stronger.

29

Do You Remember the Day Your Youth Died?

Genda is dead.

The last of my arch enemies is gone. But his descendants have established a beachhead on Molokai.

The war continues. . .

In the spring of 1945, the Japanese war machine was crumbling. They were being driven back on all fronts. The final revenge for Pearl Harbor was near. I was helping.

Every afternoon at 2:40 p.m., right after two Our Fathers, three Hail Marys, and "My Country 'Tis of Thee" in Sister Petrie's first grade class at Sacred Heart, I'd run home the long way to avoid the Brindel twins— the original role models for the Shiite terrorists. I'd shed my civilian attire for full combat gear—the plastic version of the official U.S. Marine Corps helmet, galoshes doubling as combat boots, a Red Ryder BB gun with rubber bayonet, a Captain Midnight walkie-talkie, and four small beanbags pressed into service as hand grenades.

"Where ya goin', Bobby?"

Mom always knew where I was going, but I guess mothers have this duty to ask anyway.

"Guadalcanal, Iwo Jima, and Saipan," I smartly replied.

She never broke stride from her dusting.

"Fine. Don't get hurt. Be home by five for dinner."

Mothers don't understand war.

Since 1942, I had fought in every major campaign in World War II. As far as I could tell, I was the only seven-year-old three-time winner of the Congressional Medal of Honor who had served with distinction in all three services in both Europe and the Pacific and who had, single-handedly, run Rommel out of the Sahara, memorized every line of dialogue from every Randolph Scott war movie, and— under the threat of excommunication from the Catholic Church—made a vow to the Almighty to personally seek out and destroy every Japanese planner of the dastardly sneak attack at Pearl.

Today, during recess, I had broken the enemy's code. I knew that Genda and Fuchida, the two sons of the devil who masterminded the attack, were visiting ground troops in the Pacific. I didn't know where, but I was prepared to fight across every island, atoll, and coral reef west of the 157th parallel. I laid in heavy siege supplies in my 50-caliber ammo Thom McAnn shoe box—two cream cheese and jelly and one liverwurst sandwich, canteen full of lime Kool-Aid.

Mom seemed preoccupied with small things. She didn't realize this could be our final goodbye. I didn't have the heart to tell her.

I walked across the street to "Guadalcanal," a half-acre field of scrub brush, elephant grass, and abandoned

'32 Chevys. The place was filled with Japanese pillboxes. They had doubled their patrols today, probably to protect their sneaky visiting VIPs. My entire battalion had been wiped out ten days ago, just before I got wounded. (My school nurse said chicken pox, but I knew it was shrapnel from a Jap mortar shell.) I was back now, and I was alone.

I went to my secret spot, pulled back the camouflage, and there she was, "Blood and Guts Gertie."

Dad was the best scrap lumber designer-builder in Glendale, New York. He could take Mrs. Blasky's rusty breadbox, Mom's broom handle, Uncle Al's cigar box, and the frame from Grandpa's old umbrella and make a perfect 50-caliber machine gun that did more to keep America free than all the war bonds ever sold.

Today I write on the gun barrel, "Get Genda."

Outgunned and outmanned, I fought every day from three to five, seven days a week. I got close a few times. Thought I wounded him on Saipan during a daring daylight raid on the Japanese high command, but he got away.

In late August, Mom said she needed her broom handle. The Japanese had surrendered. I could only look at it, now standing in the hall closet, the fading red crayon words reminding me of my failed mission in life, "Get Genda."

But fate is kind to young patriots.

I grew up to become a naval officer at Pearl Harbor in charge of public relations. I read every book, looked at every photograph, interviewed every survivor, and memorized the face and battle résumé of every senior Japanese officer in the war. The Navy called me an expert and frequently had me give visiting dignitaries a "lively" escorted tour of the historic harbor. When the visitors were Japanese, my Admiral made it a point to look me squarely in the eye and admonish me, "Remember, the war is over. They're our allies now."

The war is never over for a three-time Medal of Honor winner.

As I was walking down to the boat landing to take a "Japanese Minister" on tour, I got that old feeling I used to get on "Guadalcanal" when I sensed unseen enemy snipers targeting my machine gun nest. Something was up.

The "minister" bowed. Before he raised his head to reveal his face, I knew all good things come to he who waits. He stood up and I was face to face with Matsuo Fuchida, the man who had led the aerial attack on Pearl Harbor.

The little boy said, "Attack. Go for the throat. Wrestle him to the ground. Watch out for that knife undoubtedly hidden in his pants leg. Sidestep his quick judo moves and land a Randolph Scott haymaker to his bony jaw."

The man side said, "Cool it! Facing a firing squad two months before discharge would really upset Mom."

The man side won.

He read my disdain and volunteered a fantastic story. "I felt the need to do penance after the war. So I became a fundamentalist minister, moved to Seattle, married an American, and had two daughters."

I wasn't sure which part was the penance. I clenched my teeth, listened patiently, and then refused to let him step onboard the Arizona Memorial. I had to. I would never be able to face my little boy again.

He seemed to understand, smiled faintly, and turned to leave.

I deadpanned, "Where's Genda?"

That stopped him dead in his tracks. He turned slowly, lost the battle to see which one of us would blink first, shrugged his shoulders, and left.

All these far-away things suddenly alive again. Why?

Because I'm spread out in my favorite sit-and-do-nothing place, the creaky ancient porch of the venerable Maunaloa Plantation Store on top of a red hill on the dry west end of the island, thirty-four miles from the tree-house.

Because I've just read a short two-paragraph article buried between a hemorrhoid ad and an announcement for a Filipino bake sale on page A10 of the *Maui News*:

Attack Planner Dies

TOKYO—Minoru Genda, a chief planner of Japan's surprise attack on Pearl Harbor and a former member of Parliament, died yesterday, the anniversary of Japan's surrender in World War II. He would have been 85 today.

His family said Genda died of a heart attack in a hospital.

I'd like to think he died from an old war wound suffered in a spectacular one-man predawn attack on Japanese headquarters in 1945.

I mark the time and date. August 20, 3:31 p.m. I have finally put away all the things of my youth.

30

The Rising Sun Casts a Giant Shadow

Still at the Maunaloa store.

Irony and absurdity are easy companions today. Below me are 6,000 acres, once lush prime cattle pastureland, sitting at the very edge of the island and bounded on three sides by beyond-breathtaking vistas of the Pacific. Now it is just a huge checkerboard of marked-off homesites and mounds of construction debris.

Price tag:	$30,000,000.00
Buyers:	Japanese
Intent:	Page one of my three-day-old paper carries the answer in its headline, one that may prove more devastating to the pursuit of world sanity than the one on December 7, 1941:

Japanese Intend to Build Up Molokai
to Rival Waikiki Beach

Our old adversaries have returned to Hawaii with the most potent weapon ever imagined—a stable currency and lots of it.

Their casually announced gluttony to buy every homesite, hotel, business, and parcel of exposed dirt at outrageously inflated prices has sadly validated the claim of the heartless—everyone and everything has a price.

The sale of the century is taking place in the middle of the Pacific. It's a close-out sale. Everything is going. Local owners are gorging themselves on Nippon's money, selling everything that produces income: hotels, golf courses, newspapers, banks, TV stations, ancestral lands, national heritage, everything.

Nothing is beyond the grasp of the Rising Sun. The feeding frenzy has reached into the spirit world. The Bishop of Honolulu, against the will of his flock, is considering selling his Catholic cathedral and all its inspiring ocean view lots for twice its value, about $8 million. Soon, $400-a-night hotel rooms will stand where once the largest religious community in the state prayed for the triumph of goodness over greed.

Is there nothing in the human condition that escapes the tincture of absurdity!?

Every island in the chain Robert Louis Stevenson once called, "The loveliest fleet of islands that lie anchored in any ocean" has fallen. Every island but one . . . the smallest, the poorest, and the proudest . . . Molokai.

For fifty years, the long-suffering people of the Friendly Isle have fought to keep out the profiteer's bulldozer and his plundering schemes of turning the last island paradise into a floating subdivision for jet-setting blue bloods.

They warned, "Molokai is a spiritual place. The Hawaiian gods live here and tell us to protect the aina (land) and keep the beauty blooming for future generations. Don't defile our sacred place."

"They" didn't listen. They came with their big digging machines in the late sixties. They were going to carve through the sacred mountains, dredge the ancient fishponds, and build the temples of the future called mega-resorts. The people said no, the gods would strike back with a vengeance the way they have for fourteen centuries. They laughed. When their tallest crane mysteriously fell one day and when workers were falling off platforms and suffering unexplained injuries, they stopped laughing. They left. Their tall digging machinery can still be seen, broken and rusting in the mud as the forest comes to reclaim it and turn it back into food for the aina.

Molokai is a special place. Her people know it. They've seen the local people of the other islands who bought the promise that rapid development meant progress and that meant better jobs. Now they see these same folks making plastic leis, driving tour buses, washing dishes, and cleaning toilets in overpriced gaudy palaces by the sea.

They look across the channel to Maui and its once-majestic Kaanapali coastline, home of the Hawaiian alii, now dwarfed by huddling concrete monoliths, each containing hundreds of small boxes selling for a half-million apiece. Maui, once the jewel in the crown of Polynesia, now being ground into a glitzy casbah of mini-malls strung together by T-shirt joints and one trendy neon junkyard of useless tourist chic after another. Maui, its rich agricultural land being terraced for Japanese golf courses and vacation villas for the rich and famous. Maui, a gullible innocence, betrayed, reeling under the cancer of unplanned growth—massive traffic jams, dwindling water and power supplies, unable to house its own children of the land. The one exception remains: "Heavenly" Hana on the fertile northeast tip, considered by truth seeker and romanticist alike as the most beautiful unspoiled garden on our planet.

Molokaians see all this and passionately believe that the word "progress" needs to be redefined to mean showing extraordinary care for the land in all that we do.

And they've paid dearly for that simple dedication.

You see, Molokai, protector of the real spirit of Aloha for the land, isn't allowed to govern itself like the other islands. Now here's the absurdity again. They have to beg for their tax money from the least likely guardian of common sense in the Pacific, proven losers in the battle for sensible growth . . . the county government of . . . Maui. Heroes held hostage by cowards.

I'm watching a flaming orange sun kiss the horizon and shoot blazing golden ribbons of fire across the ocean.

Gary's watching, too. He's the new forty-year-old store proprietor who left a brilliant career as a chemical engineer when his southern, sleepy Connecticut hometown suddenly became gridlocked with "progress" and his doctor said he was suffering from severe malaise.

He's a quiet man who always seems to be listening to some inner voice before speaking, consequently he only says precisely what he feels. A rare companion.

He hears that voice now. Still awed by the fiery end of day before us, he hands me a copy of today's *Maui News*, points to the headline, and whispers, "Why would anyone want to destroy all this beauty?"

"Japanese Real Estate Firm Buys 4,500 Acres of Heavenly Hana. What's Next?"

We both know the answer but prefer to face the fading sun in quiet appreciation of the moment. Tiny Molokai, the last island, faces its final battle for survival.

And so am I. Next morning. . .

I'm rocked out of bed by a loud, hideous caterwauling sound that's vibrating every organ of my body along with the quarter-inch slats in the treehouse. Got to be the Four Horsemen of the Apocalypse announcing the arrival of Armageddon.

Close.

It's Mr. Buelli, the occasional yard man. He's grinning and pointing to the end of Paradise in the Pacific.

"My new leef blo'er. Jest came from da mainland. Whatdayatink?"

I "tink" I could probably get off with justifiable homicide.

31

Aloha, Molokai!

Sunday, 6:40 a.m.

My last day.

Summer is fighting a losing battle with fall for control of the skies. Low thick ribbons of gray crisscross the Pacific and seem to press down hard on the horizon. The softness of the trades is gone. The wind is anxious, cold, relentless.

Take a swim out to breakers. Fighting the strongest current I've felt since arriving.

The heart and soul of the Pacific is changing. Its name now seems most inappropriate.

A few miles out in the shipping lanes a black tug with a Teddy Roosevelt mustache is pulling a big, lazy giant bound for Maui. At the wheel is a bear of a man, salty, free, content, on course, munching on a Lorna Doone.

There is a great stirring going on. Space, air, light, and the leaf are all changing color and tone, while dancing whitecaps monopolize the channel, celebrating the rhythm of a new season. Nothing seems the same.

It's hard to tell in nature if what you're seeing is a beginning or an ending. You can call it either. It doesn't matter. I like that.

Sitting at John Muir's grave just watching the new tapestry unfold. No thoughts. No searching. No voices. Just becalmed in the moment.

Can't begin to tell you how long I sat there. I do remember when I left. Just a few seconds after a thought visited me. A simple one from one of Emerson's essays that will forever answer my doubts on anything:

"Give me health and a day and I will make the pomp of emperors ridiculous."

I have both.

Thank you, Molokai, and aloha!

Oh, P.S.—Before I leave, at least one mystery of the universe will be answered for me.

I arrive at the Hoolehua airport an hour early for my eighteen-minute Hawaiian Airlines flight back to another world.

The barefoot baggage handler is carrying a large, noisy metal box to the grassy knoll to the left of the one and only arrival gate. He opens the screen cover top and out fly a dozen red-footed, Jean-Harlow-white freckled toasted whole-wheat-beaked birds.

"Hey, what's going on?" I ask.

"Oh, twice a year some sign-tist guy ovah in Honolulu at da university sends dese birds over here and axs me to let 'em go. He wanna see how many are smart enough to find der way back to Honolulu. Gee, beeg waste, huh. Des all dumb pigeons. Dey nevah make it. Mongoose always eat 'em."

He searches the box, finds one shy resident, picks him up, and throws him high in the sky. Once airborne, the bird finds the wind and glides smoothly toward the Pu'u Nana mountains to the west, into the setting sun.

"Every year I bet dis guy not one of dem dumb buggahs gonna make it back." All 300 pounds of him starts laughing at once, ". . .and every year I ween."

Not this year, my friend. Definitely not this year.

Epilogue

What I Learned in the Treehouse

- Don't be fooled into thinking life is a mystical search for meaning. Life is only one instant of consciousness. That's all. If you use it wisely, it's enough.

- Stop mourning the loss of heroes. Be one yourself. Start bellowing. If you don't like the loss of basic values sweeping the land, then stop doing nothing. Stand. Protest. Write letters. Be a Minuteman. Do something now. Then join a lot of other people who feel the same way, and keep shouting. Face reality. You've got to be an aggressive advocate in this new age dawning. The media favors the crowd that makes the most noise. And all our battles for a return to sanity will be fought in the media. Get crackin'. Start bellowing!

- There is a cartoon lurking inside of every tragedy. Find it. Ultimately your health depends upon it.

- Put a rainbow over everybody you know. When they start to bug you, look at the rainbow.

- If your life doesn't feel good, you're dying. Change lots of things.

- Never let a doctor have the last word. Listen to your body. It's always talking. It'll tell you what's wrong. Then listen to your little voices for the treatment.

- Don't ever admit you're sick. The body is very impressionable. It believes everything you tell it.

- Cities have no power to heal. Take a walk in the woods.

- Listen to the waves.

- Question every real estate developer's plans.

- If someone you know says they're bored with life, walk away from them and don't look back.

- The best stress management is to shout "time out!" Do nothing. Listen. Keep a yellow pad and pencil handy. Write down the answers; they'll come.

- Stop trying to find yourself. You're not lost. Commit to the thing you love. Do it with gusto. That's you.

- Hum as often as you can. It tells the rest of your body everything's okay.

- If you find yourself rushing anywhere, stop. Take a deep breath and say three times, "It's not that important."

- Change every routine you have. Start an adventurer's club. Be the only member. Every day do two things you've never done before. Use a new word. Go to a different church. Simple stuff like that.

- Every politician who doesn't act as if preserving the environment is priority number one should be booted out of office, pronto.

- Paradise is not a place but an idea you carry around with you.

- Fear is a greater teacher than reason. Humanity will not suddenly wake up one day and start to care. Only global catastrophe and great personal pain will change people. Shine a light, but don't try to make people hold your flashlight.

- Plant flowers every chance you get.

- My mother and father were right . . . about everything.

- Fifty is learning you've been flying without a parachute all along. Stop looking for safe landings. There aren't any. Everybody falls. So quit your kicking and just fly like a bird. Lighten up and win!

- Think like a cat. Don't gripe and moan. Just accept the immediate reality you're facing.

- Everybody needs a treehouse.

Helpful Hints for Other 50-Year-Olds Seeking a Treehouse

- Don't look for a sanctuary. Let it find you. It's already in your heart. Listen for the directions.

- Pick the high ground. In nature, inspiration is directly proportional to elevation.

- Talk with your "voices." Remember, they're all dictators with no listening skills. Teach them your life is a two-way conversation, and majority rules.

- Read only the uplifting authors.

- Read your Bible in the woods. That's where it was meant to be read.

- Don't plan your days. Let them happen.

- Get up before sunrise every day and experience morning.

- Walk in the rain as often as possible.

- Erase expectation. Anticipate nothing. Have no guilt about being lazy. Doing nothing is where all the learning starts.
- Be especially kind to old people.
- Don't try to "befriend" any creature small or tall. Be alone for a while. Lose your city ways. They'll find you.
- Read no paper. Watch no television. Sing a lot.
- Write to your mother. And bring a large bottle of Pepto Bismol.